AWAKE O. DEBORAH AND SING

*Anointed Women Arise
And Discover Their Destiny*

Scott McConaughey

PRESS

DEDICATIONS

I dedicate this book to the amazing women in my life who
inspire me to sing my song.

To my beloved wife Glenda
who truly is a Proverbs 31 woman!

To our amazing five daughters, Christine,
Mary, Rachel, Elizabeth and Rebecca,
who all prophesy and walk by the Spirit.

To our pastor, Sally Beckmann,
who is a last-day Deborah and a friend of God.

To all the Deborahs who are awakening to sing their songs.

To find out more about the author's ministry
and other resources please contact:

Living Waters School of Ministry
Pastor Scott McConaughey
scottmcconaughey@sbcglobal.net
www.scottmc.org/ (see resources)

TABLE OF CONTENTS

INTRODUCTION

Now this is the main point of the things we are saying: We have such a High Priest, who is seated at the right hand of the throne of the Majesty in the heavens, a Minister of the sanctuary and of the true tabernacle which the Lord erected, and not man. For every high priest is appointed to offer both gifts and sacrifices. Therefore it is necessary that this One also have something to offer. For if He were on earth, He would not be a priest, since there are priests who offer the gifts according to the law; who serve <u>the copy and shadow</u> of the heavenly things, as Moses was divinely instructed when he was about to make the tabernacle. For He said, "See that you make all things according to the pattern shown you on the mountain." But now He has obtained a more excellent ministry, inasmuch as He is also Mediator of a better covenant, which was established on better promises. Hebrews 8:1-6 (underlining mine)

According to this passage in Hebrews, the tabernacle Moses built was a copy and shadow of spiritual realities in heavenly places. The natural tabernacle on Earth was a prophetic picture of a spiritual tabernacle in heaven. New Testament priests do not enter into the tabernacle of Moses but are graced by God to enter into the true tabernacle of heaven.

There are many prophetic pictures with types and shadows throughout the Bible. The story of Deborah is a type and a shadow of what God is going to do through women leaders in the last-day Church. Deborah is also an excellent picture of the warrior bride of Christ emerging in this hour.

The revelation of Deborah came to me by the Spirit in a unique way. In 2001, I was asked to speak at a meeting that was once part of the Women's Aglow movement. The hostess told me that the meeting would be attended primarily by older women. As I prayed and prayed over this meeting, the Spirit took me into the revelation of Deborah, and He led me to preach part of the message in this book with great unction for nearly two hours! Even though I was only preaching to twenty "little old ladies" and a few older gentlemen, the Spirit was very firm that I preach the message with all my heart and with fairly intense volume. The title of my message, **"Awake O Deborah and Sing"** was rather prophetic as some of the senior patrons were rather dozy.

As I prayed individually over the older women in the prayer line, I came to a lively old gentleman. When I looked into his blazing eyes, I said frankly, "You need to pray for me!" This older prophet had an intimate relationship with Jesus. He was so excited by my message on Deborah that he practically jumped up and down on his seat for the entire two hours that I preached. He told me that God put that message in his heart many years ago and that he was so happy to hear me release it. The man of God prayed for me and I received a prophet's blessing that day. This gave me another confirmation that the word about Deborah was accurate.

Mysteriously, the Lord never had me release that word again in any other setting. The word just sat in my heart for over a year. Then I was asked to bring two messages on women in ministry but the Lord did not lead me to speak on Deborah at all. He directed me to speak on the theology of women in ministry. After that, the Lord spoke to my heart,

"The woman overcomes the dragon" (see Revelation 13:13-17). I knew by His Spirit that He wanted me to pursue writing this book to set captives free who have been persecuted by the enemy and held back from ministry. When anointed women fully arise and are released to advance God's kingdom in agreement with anointed men, the devil's kingdom will be overcome.

Examples in the Bible

Now these things became our examples, to the intent that we should not lust after evil things as they also lusted. And do not become idolaters as were some of them. As it is written, "The people sat down to eat and drink, and rose up to play." Nor let us commit sexual immorality, as some of them did, and in one day twenty-three thousand fell; nor let us tempt Christ, as some of them also tempted, and were destroyed by serpents; nor complain, as some of them also complained, and were destroyed by the destroyer. Now all these things happened to them as examples, and they were written for our admonition, on whom the ends of the ages have come. I Corinthians 10:6-11

The Old Testament is filled with stories that are examples to us. The life of Deborah gives us an example of how God wants to use women in ministry today. Deborah was a woman leader who lived in an ancient world dominated by men! Deborah was chosen by God to be the judge over the entire nation of Israel. This remarkable woman brought the land into peace for forty years.

God can and does choose women today to be leaders over churches, cities and nations. God anoints them with an endowment of the Holy Spirit so they can do His assignment. Deborah was so anointed by God that the powerful general Barak would not think of going to battle without her. The nation saw the favor of God on Deborah and no man made an objection to her leadership. She was a great mother in Israel and a powerful example to all women.

The Natural Comes First and Afterward the Spiritual

It is sown a natural body, it is raised a spiritual body. There is a natural body, and there is a spiritual body. And so it is written, "The first man Adam became a living being." The last Adam became a life-giving spirit. However, the spiritual is not first, but the natural, and afterward the spiritual. The first man was of the earth, made of dust; the second Man is the Lord from heaven. As was the man of dust, so also are those who are made of dust; and as is the heavenly Man, so also are those who are heavenly. And as we have borne the image of the man of dust, we shall also bear the image of the heavenly Man. I Corinthians 15:44-49

The entire Old Testament deals with the history of natural Israel. The natural corporate son, Israel, came first. The spiritual corporate son, the Church, comes after the natural. God taught His laws to govern the nation of Hebrews living in the Promised Land known as Israel. Joshua had to lead men into violent warfare in order to take hold of the Promised Land and drive out natural enemies. Most of the Old Testament stories speak of natural realm events. We have to learn lessons from the Old Testament and apply them to spiritual realities in the Church. We have to drive out spiritual enemies with spiritual weapons in order to possess the Promised Land of our inheritance.

Deborah was a real woman prophetess who led Barak and an army of at least 10,000 into a real war against Sisera and 900 chariots of iron. There was a God-sent natural phenomenon of intense rain with a flash flood that caused the chariots to get stuck in the mud in the Kishon valley. A real woman named Jael took a tent peg and pounded it through the head of Sisera and killed him. Everything we read in Judges 4 about Deborah had a fulfillment in the natural realm. However, nearly everything also has a prophetic meaning, especially the prophetic song in Judges 5. Women will have to rise up like Deborah and fight spiritual warfare battles so that they can be birthed into the ministry positions God has for them. This will happen through prophetic intercession including worship, praise and prophetic actions.

There are many millions of women in captivity to man's oppression in the world right now. Most religions oppress women severely and do not allow them to even sit with men. There is a gross double standard in Islam and Asian religions when it comes to women. God wants to deliver millions of Muslim and Asian women along with men. Christianity is the "religion" of Jesus Christ, the Son of God. Jesus liberated women in an extraordinary manner during His public ministry. He wants us to liberate and equip women to be anointed last-day warriors in the Spirit as Deborah was in the natural.

Now Deborah

Now Deborah, a prophetess, the wife of Lapidoth, was judging Israel at that time. And she would sit under the palm tree of Deborah between Ramah and Bethel in the mountains of Ephraim. And the children of Israel came up to her for judgment. Judges 4:4,5

Deborah is the fourth judge listed in the book of Judges. The prophetic anointing on this woman was extraordinarily powerful. The nation of Israel recognized the anointing on Deborah and went to her to hear the word of the Lord, receive counsel and decide matters of national importance. Deborah was God's appointed national leader for the nation of Israel for four decades.

Deborah was married and recognized as a prophetess. Men, like Barak, submitted to her leadership. As a judge, Deborah was called to lead the people out of idolatry into true worship and obedience to God. This amazing woman was appointed by God to lead a nation, and she did so with great success. Deborah inspired the male army into violent battle against those who were allowed to oppress them because of Israel's idolatry. Deborah and Barak led the army to defeat the wicked king Jabin and his general, Sisera. Under Deborah's outstanding leadership, the land came into peace for forty years.

Deborah is a prophetic picture of what God is going to do through women who are anointed by God to operate in government offices of the Church. This includes the offices of apostle, prophet, pastor, teacher and evangelist. These five-fold offices have authority to govern the Church and advance God's kingdom on Earth.

Men have been readily accepted as leaders in the Church. Women have been predominantly excluded from positions of Church government, and a strong theology has been developed that leads most Christians to believe that women are not supposed to be in places of Church government.

Challenges come to our religious traditions when God powerfully anoints women, speaks to them profoundly and uses them quite dramatically to minister the word of God, heal the sick, deliver the demonized and win souls to Christ. God is anointing women and calling them into positions of leadership in the Church. Since the vast majority of the senior pastors of churches are men, the rise of anointed women is leading many men to take a closer look at their theology about women in ministry. This book will help men and women understand God's intent from the very beginning.

Deborah was an anointed woman and was recognized as a national judge. There was no prohibition for Deborah judging the nation whose history was dominated by men in leadership. Men submitted to her leadership because of the anointing upon her. Men today have difficulty submitting to women in leadership because of a theology that believes that a woman should not take authority over a man. This is based on a few verses that Paul wrote. We will examine these verses and many others in this book.

Jesus Comes in New Forms

Several years ago a woman prophet walked into our home to speak to a group of Christians that had gathered. God spoke to this woman about the intense spiritual warfare that was going on in our area, and He sent her through some phone contacts to our house. When this anointed prophet walked into the room, I heard the Spirit say, **"This is Jesus in a new form."** The woman spoke to our group, and we listened intently to what she had to say because it was the word of the Lord.

There was an intense demonic presence in our home that night and I knew that presence was in the corner of our living room behind an uninvited guest. During her talk, the prophet stopped, looked at that exact corner and said, "There's a demonic spirit standing in that corner." The prophet pointed her finger at the intruder, commanded it to leave, and the dark presence immediately left the room much to my relief. I said to myself, "I have to get to know this woman." God appointed that meeting and today I serve under the leadership of that prophet whom we call Pastor Sally Beckmann of Living Waters Fellowship in Barstow, California.

I did not have a theology to submit to a woman pastor. I once strongly believed that only men could be leaders in matters of Church government. As a missionary and pastor for many years, we involved women in ministry, but not in any leadership over a man. When I met Pastor Sally, I did have enough sense to recognize the anointing, authority and the power of the Lord in which she walked. I also heard the Lord speak to my heart, "This is Jesus in a new form."

After that, He appeared <u>in another form</u> to two of them as they walked and went into the country. And they went and told it to the rest, but they did not believe them either. Later He appeared to the eleven as they sat at the table; and He rebuked their unbelief and hardness of heart, because they did not believe those who had seen Him after He had risen. Mark 16:12-14 (underlining mine)

After Jesus rose from the dead, He appeared in another form to the two who walked with Him on the road to Emmaus. As they looked at the Man in the natural, they could not recognize Him. But when He opened their eyes in the breaking of bread, they knew it was Jesus (see Luke 24:13-35).

Previously, Jesus had appeared to Mary Magdalene and other women who did not immediately recognize Him either. Mary thought Jesus was the gardener (John 20:15). Jesus' first post resurrection appearance was to women. He gave them a word to take to the men and they gladly ran to tell Jesus' eleven disciples the word (Matthew 28:7,8).

Then they returned from the tomb and told all these things to the eleven and to all the rest. It was Mary Magdalene, Joanna, Mary the mother of James, and the other women with them, who told these things to the apostles. And their words seemed to them like idle tales, and they did not believe them. Luke 24:9-12

The apostles also rejected the word from the women disciples who had seen and heard the risen Christ. They rejected the word from the two witnesses. When Jesus appeared to the eleven, He rebuked them for their unbelief and hardness of heart because they did not believe the women or the two men. Why did the eleven have trouble believing the women? It was simply because Jesus came in another form. The apostles did not think that Jesus would give a word to women. They must have reasoned that if Jesus were to appear to anyone, He would have appeared to them first. After all, they were His chosen apostles, and they were men!

Peter, as the anointed leader of the Church after Pentecost, did not think it possible that God would bring salvation to anyone except the Jews. God had to show Peter in a trance that His good news was for everyone (see Acts 10:9-48). **"Then Peter opened his mouth, and said, of a truth I perceive that God is no respecter of persons" (Acts 10:34 KJV).** Peter recognized that God is no respecter of persons. He realized the truth, we take for granted, that every person of every race can receive salvation through faith in Jesus Christ. Paul recognized that every person can become a **"son of God"** through faith in Christ Jesus (see Galatians 3:26-28).

Peter and the other ten were awesome men of God whom God used mightily. They did not believe God would appear to women or bring the gospel to the Gentiles. They were wrong. The Lord rebuked them. They repented and moved on.

There are many awesome men of God leading churches today who are similar to the Lord's eleven after the resurrection. Most men in leadership still don't think Jesus would speak to women and appoint them to leadership roles in the Church. Just as Peter and the other apostles once thought it was impossible then for women to have a word from the Lord, so it is today. Jesus is going to speak to many men and rebuke them in their unbelief and hardness of heart related to women being in ministry. Jesus is appearing in a new form, and that form is through anointed women whom He is

17

choosing to place in positions of Church leadership.

God has already anointed many women in the last century who have battled to be accepted in the Church. Most have never been allowed to be a part of Church government, and this has hindered our churches from becoming what Christ has intended them to become. It is clear that God is anointing women. He is moving in new forms. Our eyes need to be opened to see the truth that God has always intended, that women rule alongside men in Church government. While this truth has been mostly veiled for the past two thousand years, we are now entering into the third thousand years since Christ walked on Earth. Many are calling this the third-day Church that will walk in resurrection power.

On the third day, Jesus appeared to women first. On the third day, Jesus was influenced by His mother to turn water into wine. On the third day, Jesus is perfected in His body. We are going to carefully examine the theology of women in ministry.

In September of 2000, I joined my wife Glenda and Pastor Sally as they attended the Women of Destiny Conference in Los Angeles hosted by Cindy Jacobs. Those three days had a powerful influence on our lives and I bless God for Cindy Jacobs and the team that presented scriptures to us about women in ministry. I carefully read Cindy's book, **WOMEN OF DESTINY**, and used notes from Dr. Gary Grieg's presentation on women as aids in this work. God has shown me many other things as I have prayed and waited on Him during the last years. I present these to you readers with the prayer that God would open your eyes to the awakening of Deborah, the rise of women in ministry and the powerful blessing it is indeed!

CHAPTER 1

GOD GAVE "THEM" DOMINION

Then God said, "Let Us make man in Our image, according to Our likeness; let them have dominion over the fish of the sea, over the birds of the air, and over the cattle, over all the earth and over every creeping thing that creeps on the earth." So God created man in His own image; in the image of God He created him; male and female He created <u>them</u>. Then God blessed <u>them</u>, and God said to <u>them</u>, "Be fruitful and multiply; fill the earth and subdue it; have dominion over the fish of the sea, over the birds of the air, and over every living thing that moves on the earth." Genesis 1:26-28 (underlining mine)

God created mankind in His own image; male and female He created them. God is pure Spirit who is composed of all the redemptive qualities of male and female. The Holy trinity of God is not three male persons that exclude all female characteristics. The Holy Spirit has many motherly characteristics and is referred to as "she" in Proverbs 8. The Father, Son and Holy Spirit incorporate all the holy qualities of male and female represented as "His image" in Adam and Eve in their pure state.

God created "them" to be His representative head over the earth. God's command to "them," the first couple, was to exercise righteous dominion over everything on the earth in the power of holy, loving agreement. Genesis 1:26-28 establishes God's purpose in creation. He created them to be like Him, a trinitarian being, Father, Son and Holy Spirit, who exercises dominion in perfect agreement.

Assuredly, I say to you, whatever you bind on earth will be bound in heaven, and whatever you loose on earth will be loosed in heaven. Again I say to you that if two of you agree on earth concerning anything that they ask, it will be done for them by My Father in heaven. For where two or three are gathered together in My name, I am there in the midst of them. Matthew 18:18-20

Jesus taught us about the tremendous power believers have in pure agreement. God wants us to take dominion over our families to protect them from the assaults of evil. God wants His disciples to walk in dominion over sickness, disease and darkness. He wants us to rule and reign with Christ. This is only possible as we walk together in agreement with Him and others in the body of Christ. This is especially true as men and women walk in mature agreement.

God created "them" in His own image; male and female He created them. The male gender has essential and vital qualities of God. The female gender also has essential and vital qualities of God. Neither male nor female can fully represent the image of God independently. As men and women submit to the Holy Spirit and grow in grace in a loving community, they will corporately reflect the image of God.

God said that they were to exercise dominion over the fish in the sea, the living creatures on land and the birds in the air. While God intended Adam and Eve to have a natural realm dominion, He wants the Church to have spiritual realm dominion as well. Fish represent demonic creatures under the earth. Living things represent demonic entities on the earth and birds represent principalities and spiritual forces of Satan that seek to rule in the atmosphere over the earth. We are to have dominion over all three levels of demonic influence on the earth. This cannot happen apart from a righteous agreement between men and women in Church government.

Dominion

You have made him to have dominion over the works of Your hands; You have put all things under his feet. Psalm 8:6

David was amazed at the grace God gave mankind to have dominion over all the works of His hands on Earth. God set an order that mankind was to have the rule on Earth. That order was for "them" to have dominion. Dominion means "control or the exercise of control; to rule or have sovereignty over."

Biblical dominion is a positive word. Picture a husband and wife bringing home their first-born child from the hospital. The parents have complete and absolute dominion over the life of that little child. The infant is completely dependent upon her parents for food, nourishment, clothing, cleansing and safety. When parents exercise their dominion in love and righteousness, the child grows to become a healthy, well-adjusted adult. If the parents abuse that dominion, the child will suffer greatly.

God intended Adam and Eve to exercise a benevolent dominion of stewardship authority over the planet. They could only do this in the power of perfect agreement as long as they operated by the anointing of the Holy Spirit symbolized in the tree of life. If they disobeyed God's commandment and ate from the tree of the knowledge of good and evil, they would be cut off from God's anointing and lose their ability to exercise dominion.

The tree of the knowledge of good and evil represents the freewill choice to operate by ones own standard of what is good and evil rather than operating by God's standards. Doctrines of Pharisees come from intellectual understandings of the word of God rather than revelation understanding by the Holy Spirit. Many "Christians" are living by natural reason rather than by revelation of the things of the Spirit. Consequently, man's doctrine has opposed the doctrines of the Holy Spirit. This is true in doctrines of Church government related to women.

God called "them" to have dominion. "Them" was a man and a woman in loving agreement, walking in the purity of God's anointing. Adam was the appointed head but could only have dominion in agreement with Eve. Once they fell, through deception and rebellion, they no longer had the capacity to exercise dominion and fulfill God's mandate.

Just as Adam could not rule in dominion over the earth without the agreement of Eve, Jesus Christ will not rule in full dominion over the earth without the agreement of His bride, the Church. The fulfillment of God's command to have dominion is only possible now through faith in Jesus Christ as men and women mature to the place where they walk in perfect agreement with the Holy Spirit and His anointing. God intends to mature the Church so that she can be a coregent with Christ on the earth. As men and women in the Church come into greater agreement and abide in the anointing, she will grow into higher levels of dominion authority over sickness, demons and wickedness on Earth until Christ comes.

Agreement at Home

"Can two walk together, unless they are agreed?" (**Amos 3:3**). God has greatly blessed my wife Glenda and me with powerful agreement. Coming from different countries, we joined the same mission field at a young age, developed a friendship, then fell in love and married. We began raising our children on the mission field in the inner city of St. Louis. We lived in a poor neighborhood on the north side and observed a great deal of domestic violence. Only one in fifteen families that we ministered to had a father and mother living together. All the other homes were "broken." Some were more broken than others.

Satan has conspired to destroy the agreement between husband and wife, male and female. The results of broken relationships in urban homes is devastating to children and the society. We ministered the love of God to many insecure and deeply wounded children. I could tell you many stories of the heartache little boys and girls experienced as they saw a drunken man, possibly their father, rage and beat their mother. Some teenage mothers turned their children over to Grandma so they could continue to party, have sex and make more babies out of wedlock. It was not uncommon to minister to a family whose children all had different "fathers," while none actually lived in the home. A single parent in a broken home can rarely exercise dominion to keep evil out of the children's lives.

There are many Christian women in the Church whose husbands do not believe in Christ nor are they willing to submit to Him. The unbelieving husband may occasionally attend church and appear pleasant, but his heart is far from Christ. It will be extremely difficult for this couple to come into the agreement needed to exercise benevolent dominion over their children.

Some Christian couples are unequally yoked in terms of their commitment to the Lord. More often than not, it is the woman who runs after God while the husband walks with a limp. He can often become frustrated with his wife's enthusiasm and try to reel her in with various comments and body language. Unfortunately, many men can get into control at this point and resist the Holy Spirit's working in their spouse. This causes another breech in agreement.

Satan is a wicked, deviant mastermind destroyer. He realizes that the power of agreement between a husband and wife can exercise a dominion over his kingdom, and he assaults marriages relentlessly to get them out of agreement. Glenda and I have strong agreement nearly all of the time. Part of the reason for that is because I have learned to be subject to my wife in the things the Holy Spirit gives her. I have learned the hard way!

While I am the head of the home, the Lord calls me to love my wife as Christ loved the Church. I must love, lead and serve my wife as Christ served the disciples. He washed their feet and laid down His life for them. He got up early to seek the Lord and taught His disciples the word of God. I need to provide loving, serving, spiritual leadership, but I am also called to submit to my wife as appropriate. In fact, the submission issue is never even an issue in our home. We both focus intently on pleasing Christ and seeking His perfect will at all times. Glenda and I compare what the Holy Spirit is showing us through scriptures, dreams, visions and words. We pray together often and have conversations about our children and household issues several times a week.

Raising six children together has been a wonderful challenge. They all attended public schools in Los Angeles County from kindergarten through high school. Because of the power of agreement that Glenda and I have been graced to maintain, all six of our children are completely on fire for Jesus and are walking pure before the Lord seeking to please Him. There is a great umbrella of protection in prayer when a couple agrees. God shows us what is about to happen to our children through dreams and other prophetic experiences. As we pray over those things and talk to our children, the Lord intervenes and the crisis does not occur or is intercepted. It is a glorious blessing to raise children in agreement. I can't imagine doing so without the power of agreeing prayer.

The Church needs the same power of agreement as a godly, whole family. We urgently need agreement between men and women in the leadership of the body of Jesus Christ. As this power of agreement grows and men and women take their roles as chosen by the Holy Spirit evidenced by His anointing, the authority and dominion of that local church will increase proportionately. This will be a blessing to the families in the church and in the society around that church.

Men Alone in Leadership is not Good

And the LORD God said, "It is not good that man should be alone; I will make him a helper comparable to him." Genesis 2:18

Genesis 2 is the specific order of the creation of man (male and female) that actually occurred before the mandate given to "them" in Genesis 1. This creation story of Adam and Eve is purposely placed after Genesis 1. This indicates that God always intended for "them," male and female, to represent his authority and reflect His nature in community, just as husband and wife are called to reflect Christ and His Church.

God spoke that it was not good for man to be alone. God did not want Adam to have leadership alone over the planet. Together, Adam and Eve faithfully represented the image of God in perfect communion and were equipped to rule. Adam was given the responsibility as the corporate head, but the first couple was to exercise dominion and procreate in righteous, loving agreement. Both Adam and Eve were individually responsible to obey God and follow His commandments. Adam was corporately responsible for the first family.

The Father, Son and Holy Spirit operate in perfect

communication and agreement at all times as one sovereign God of the universe. Adam and Eve were created in the image of God to be like Him. The biblical family is to represent Christ and the Church (see Ephesians 5:21-33). The husband is not to be alone in his leadership over the family, but he is to work in perfect, loving agreement with His wife so as to have benevolent dominion over the children as they mature.

When the children mature, as ours have, they participate more in the responsibilities and leadership of the home until God leads them to establish their own homes. Although I am the head of our household, Glenda and I shepherd our family together. I look to all our family members for input as to what the Lord is saying. On a regular basis, we seek the Lord together and wait on Him to release revelation about a certain family need. God often gives the children prophetic visions, scripture verses, words or senses of what He is saying. When the Spirit speaks through one of our children and confirms it, we will agree as a family to move in that direction.

It would be foolish of me to think that God only speaks to me because I am the head of the household. Yet many male pastors feel that way because they are the head of their local church. Some pastors are just plain insecure. They need helpers to lead and some of those helpers are going to be prophetic women who are true intercessors. Pastors need to learn to submit to the anointing on the people in their congregations, especially the women. If the senior pastor is a woman, she needs to learn to submit to the anointing on men as well as women. God is calling for pure agreement and leadership based on His anointing and calling, not gender preferences.

The Natural First and then the Spiritual

It is sown a natural body, it is raised a spiritual body. There is a natural body, and there is a spiritual body. And so it is written, "The first man Adam became a living being." The last Adam became a life-giving spirit. However, the spiritual is not first, but the natural, and afterward the spiritual. The first man was of the earth, made of dust; the second Man is the Lord from heaven. As was the man of dust, so also are those who are made of dust; and as is the heavenly Man, so also are those who are heavenly. And as we have borne the image of the man of dust, we shall also bear the image of the heavenly Man. I Corinthians 15:44-49

In perfect wisdom, God established the natural first and afterward the spiritual. We see this in Adam and Eve as God's first natural couple who are chosen to be the representative heads of the earth and exercise dominion. Adam was a picture in the natural of Jesus Christ, who is known as the second Adam, the life-giving Spirit. Eve is a prophetic picture of the Church. Adam is known as the son of God (Luke 3:38). In various places of the Old Testament, Adam and men represent the Son of God and the sonship rights of inheritance. Their leadership and authority over the corporate family is nearly always based on natural birth order and gender, that is, the first-born son received the birthright (inheritance) to take authority over the family when the father died.

Women in the Old Testament often prophetically represent the Church, the bride of Christ. Eve, the woman taken out of man is a picture of the bride of Christ being taken out of the heart of Jesus. The bride is to become one with Jesus, bone of His bone and flesh of His flesh. The bride image is clearly a female gender reference. However, no man in Church leadership would argue that the bride of Christ is

27

made up only of women.

Similarly, all Christians are known as sons of God through faith in Christ Jesus (see Galatians 3:26-28). There is no distinction between male and female in qualification to be a son of God or a bride of Christ. The issue is faith in Christ and not gender.

The Old Testament is consistently filled with men in leadership and the inheritance rights almost always goes to the first-born son. This is a portrait in the natural that points to the man, Christ Jesus, the second Adam, the "first-born" Son of God. The scriptures in the Old Testament on women consistently portray them in a submissive role as the Church is to be unto Christ. But the Church is made up of men and women and is to be led by those called and anointed by the Lord. Corporately, the Church is considered the bride of Christ, a female gender that corresponds to Jesus as the Heavenly Bridegroom. When you grasp this principle and apply it appropriately, it helps take away the gender bias that seems apparent through much of the Bible.

The Fall Broke Gender Agreement

Then the man said, "The woman whom You gave to be with me, she gave me of the tree, and I ate." Genesis 3:12

The fall of Adam and Eve into sin broke the agreement between male and female genders. Adam immediately blamed his wife and even God who gave him the woman. Adam and Eve felt fearful, naked and ashamed in their fallen condition. They hid from God and blamed others for their transgression.

The Bible teaches us that only Eve was deceived (I Timothy 2:14). Adam transgressed (Romans 5:14). Eve was deceived into sinning but Adam willfully ate because his wife gave him the fruit. Even though Adam knew it was against

God's will, he ate anyway and was held responsible for his rebellion. Deception and rebellion are the two roots of sin today as every day. Eve was deceived and Adam transgressed.

There is a general characteristic implied here between the genders of females and males. Women tend to be deceived into sin whereas men tend to rebel and choose sin. While the characteristics apply to both genders, women can help men to submit and men can help women not be deceived.

The consequence of the fall was a great division between the first couple and subsequent gender divisions for thousands of years. They lost the power of agreement and their own family began to disintegrate when Cain rose up in murderous rage to kill Abel. The downward spiral of degeneration captivated all of the earth's inhabitants save Noah and his family.

The Results of the Fall

And I will put enmity between you and the woman, and between your seed and her Seed; He shall bruise your head, and you shall bruise His heel. To the woman He said: "I will greatly multiply your sorrow and your conception; in pain you shall bring forth children; your desire shall be for your husband, and he shall rule over you." Genesis 3:15-16

God declared an enmity between Satan and the woman. We note that the issue was to be between Satan's seed and the woman's Seed. Adam is not given the place of leadership in this war, rather it is given to the woman Eve. This is because Eve is a picture of Israel who brings forth the Seed of Jesus Christ, born of a woman. Jesus Christ has a body, known as the Church, and His seed is in her (I John 3:9). The seed of Christ is manifested on the earth in a woman, the bride of Christ. The feet of the bride are apostles and prophets who take the brunt of satanic bruising. But the feet of the bride are ultimately empowered to crush Satan. **"And the God of peace will crush Satan under your feet shortly" (Romans 16:20a).**

Jesus could easily defeat Satan from the court of heaven simply by speaking a word. Jesus already came as a man and personally defeated Satan by living a holy and blameless life. Jesus took back the keys of death and of Hades. Now Jesus intends to mature His bride so that she can reign and rule with Him. Her assignment is to mature so as to crush Satan under her feet. Jesus destroyed the works of the devil in the "legal realm." We are now called to enforce what Jesus has accomplished in the spiritual and natural realms.

And Barak said to her, "If you will go with me, then I will go; but if you will not go with me, I will not go!" Judges 4:8

Barak is a picture of the Commander and Chief of the armies of Heaven. While Jesus Christ could easily destroy Satan and his armies, the Lord does not want to go without His mature bride, His Deborah. Many Christians think that we do not have to fight in spiritual warfare because Jesus has already done everything. If Jesus had already done everything, then Satan would be out of business and the world would be a perfect place to live. Jesus accomplished His mission to gain back the dominion rights of man over Satan on the earth. Jesus did what Adam and Eve failed to do and Satan unrighteously worked to get Jesus killed. Jesus' sacrifice paid the price so that man could regain the place Adam and Eve once had in perfect agreement.

Jesus' finished work on the cross makes it possible for men and women to come back together in holy, loving agreement to exercise benevolent dominion on Earth as they walk by faith in Christ and by His anointing. We have to mature back to this place in the midst of much resistance.

The anointing of the Holy Spirit today is the Spirit of

Christ that we might prophetically say represents the second Adam. The Church of Jesus Christ, the woman, is the second Eve from a prophetic viewpoint. The Church is made up of people from various nationalities, economic levels, ages and genders. For the Church to become one with Christ in dominion, Church government needs men and women to be in complete agreement and walk by the Holy Spirit, the Spirit of Christ. So we see a restoration Adam (the Spirit of Christ, flowing from the Head, Jesus) and Eve (the body/bride of Jesus Christ) operating on the earth in pure loving agreement to reign and rule in perfect dominion.

A significant difficulty in understanding the word of God comes when teachers operate apart from the anointing of the Holy Spirit and study the Bible with their natural minds. The two on the road to Emmaus did not recognize Jesus even though the anointing was on Him powerfully to explain the scriptures. We must learn to recognize the Spirit of Christ operating by His anointing rather than by whether it is a male or female talking. As our eyes are opened to recognize the Spirit of Christ operating on a female, we can humble ourselves to submit to the anointing and to the woman God is using.

Sorrow and Pain to Women

To the woman he said, "I will greatly increase your pains in childbearing; with pain you will give birth to children. Your desire will be for your husband, and he will rule over you." Genesis 3:16 NIV

The sorrow women have experienced over the millennia is immeasurable because of the unrighteous domination of abusive men. "In pain you shall bring forth children" is true in the natural and the spiritual. It has been extremely painful for women's ministries to be birthed in the kingdom of God.

The labor pains of a woman trying to follow the anointing of the Holy Spirit or find a place in Church government or leadership has been great because of the fall of man and the unrighteous domination of men.

"Your desire shall be for your husband." God declared that the fallen nature of a woman would bend her to yield to an unrighteous desire to prefer her husband above a relationship with God. The word "desire" also means that a woman's sinful nature would desire to be bossy and controlling.

The fall affected men deeply. "He shall rule over you" is a statement that the fallen nature of man will lead him to be abusive and controlling. Adam, after the fall, began to lord it over his wife rather than be the loving, humble servant leader God intended him to be. Men in the Church, as an aspect of the fall, tend to rule over and dominate women in the Church.

Christ died to reconcile us to Himself and to each other. He intends to reconcile the genders and break the curse of the fall from us so that women don't suffer and men don't have to labor by the sweat of their own brow. They can learn to work by the power of the Holy Spirit instead.

God intends to completely reform the Church in the last days. Part of this reformation will include the leadership of women in every aspect of Church government. The religious church may reject women in leadership. Some liberal churches have accepted women in order to be politically correct. However, the word of God clearly acknowledges a place for women in leadership as one studies it under the inspiration of the Holy Spirit with careful research.

The Lord said that the pain of birthing would be greatly increased for women. He was saying that it would be extremely hard for women to ever get back to the place they were with Adam before the fall. Prior to the fall, Adam operated in perfect, loving servanthood as the head of the family. In order for the Church to get back into perfect agreement with Jesus, we have to go through many tribulations and trials. Women have an especially difficult time because most men cannot conceive that women could be anointed by God to lead in the Church.

Jesus is coming in new forms all the time. Each form has a manifestation that makes it impossible for the natural eye to discern Jesus. We must be extremely careful and wise to discern by the Spirit what the Lord is doing. The Lord is raising women up, like He did Deborah, to governmental authority in the Church. Before the Lord returns, women and men will partner in full agreement to lead the Church based on calling and anointing only. That Church will be glorious and spotless, a pure bride prepared to wed Jesus. She will be full of many women and men, girls and boys who all love Jesus with all their hearts.

CHAPTER 2

HONOR YOUR FATHER AND YOUR MOTHER

Honor your father and your mother, that your days may be long upon the land which the LORD your God is giving you. Exodus 20:12

Honor your father and your mother, as the LORD your God has commanded you, that your days may be long, and that it may be well with you in the land which the LORD your God is giving you. Deuteronomy 5:16

God gave Moses the Ten Commandments as the foundation and table of contents to all covenant law in the Old Testament. The fifth commandment, to honor your father and your mother, is the only one of the ten to have a covenant promise attached to it. This commandment was so vital in the development of the nation that God promised to bless those who honored father and mother with long life and that it would go well with them in the Promised Land.

Again, the natural comes first and afterward the spiritual. We are to honor our natural parents who have authority over us as children. We are also to honor the spiritual parents who have authority over us as children of God. We are to honor the fathers and mothers of the faith. If we do not honor our fathers and mothers of the faith, we cannot attain the agreement of the Spirit needed to take the Promised Land of our inheritance to walk in dominion with Christ.

The fifth commandment not only represented parental authority, but it set a standard for all human authority in the nation of Israel. The laws set forth in Deuteronomy are arranged topically according to the order of topics in the Ten Commandments reviewed in Deuteronomy 5. The fifth commandment governs the topic of religious authority, civil authority and state authority. Deuteronomy 17 and 18 cover specific laws about religious, civil and state authority and fall under the category of "Honor your father and your mother." A general survey of Deuteronomy 17 and 18 reveals the laws related to the authority of judges, priests, kings and prophets. Honoring "mothers" includes honoring women when they are in a place of authority such as judges, priests, kings and prophets.

In the Old Testament, Deborah was a judge and a prophet who was recognized as a mother in Israel. **"Village life ceased, it ceased in Israel, until I, Deborah, arose, arose a mother in Israel" (Judges 5:7).** Barak and the people of Israel honored the anointing on their spiritual mother Deborah, and as a result it went well with them in the land. Sisera was defeated and the land had rest for forty years (Judges 5:31).

The principle established in the life of Deborah is that God has always intended for us to learn from God-ordained women (mothers) and submit to the anointing on them. God wants young boys to learn from their natural mothers, and God called the man Barak to learn from a spiritual mother seen in Deborah. Paul reconfirmed the fifth commandment in the New Testament (see Ephesians 6:2). Obeying the fifth commandment is a major key in experiencing the blessings of God including a healthy physical life, vital ministry life and godly prosperity.

Learn From Fathers and Mothers of the Faith

My son, hear the instruction of your father, and do not forsake the law of your mother. Proverbs 1:8

The book of Proverbs was written to impart wisdom to the people of God. Wisdom literature was written for instruction to individuals and families and for the preservation of the nation. The exhortation to hear the instruction of a father and mother is consistent in the scriptures. God has placed a deposit of wisdom in godly men and women. To receive instruction from one gender exclusive to the other would be to cut off a deposit of wisdom needed to flourish in life.

My son, keep your father's command, and do not forsake the law of your mother. Bind them continually upon your heart; tie them around your neck. When you roam, they will lead you; when you sleep, they will keep you; and when you awake, they will speak with you. For the commandment is a lamp, and the law a light; reproofs of instruction are the way of life, to keep you from the evil woman, from the flattering tongue of a seductress. Do not lust after her beauty in your heart, nor let her allure you with her eyelids. Proverbs 6:20-25

Solomon often addressed his proverbs to **"my son."** Israel is sometimes referred to as God's son (see Exodus 4:22; Hosea 11:1). This male gender is not to be taken as a bias. Women are not excluded from Solomon's proverbs or from obtaining the wisdom of God because of the **"my son"** phrase. The Lord wants boys and girls to keep their father's commands and abide by the law of their mothers. Security is built into the spirit of the child that has a godly father and mother instructing her in the ways of the Lord.

Mothers tend to provide the bulk of moral instruction that will keep the maturing teenager from the flattering tongue of the seductress. This exhortation to purity applies to both young men and women. There are certainly plenty of alluring men trying to seduce women. God establishes wisdom to those who submit to and learn from spiritual fathers and mothers.

Unfortunately, most of the inner-city children we ministered to had neither a godly father nor a godly mother. I became a spiritual father to many young people and Glenda became a spiritual mother to the same. On personal issues, I counseled the boys and men, and Glenda counseled the girls and women. In the church we planted, Glenda taught Sunday School and had some influence over the males. This is proper and righteous. God put a spiritual deposit of gold in my wife that boys and men need. She often teaches truths on a personal level with practical illustrations that hit the mark with young people and adults as well. We have been blessed with a team approach to ministry that is amazingly complimentary. If young disciples only learned from me and other male ministers, they would not be as whole or complete as they could be by learning also from Glenda and other female ministers.

"The words of King Lemuel, the utterance which his mother taught him" (Proverbs 31:1). Lemuel means "devoted to God." This king devoted himself to God and learned from the lessons his mother taught him. King Lemuel's mother taught him holiness and the righteous qualities to look for in a wife. Proverbs 31 has inspired many women to walk in the wisdom of the virtuous woman described. A mother in Israel taught these qualities, and men should submit to her instruction as they look for a godly wife.

"She speaks with wisdom, and faithful instruction is

Prov 31 to show spiritual authority?

on her tongue" (**Proverbs 31:26 NIV**). The anointed woman speaks with wisdom taught by the Spirit. Her pure heart releases faithful instruction to those who would learn from her. God places a deposit of wisdom and instruction in devoted women. The Church must learn to honor spiritual mothers and allow them a place to speak into the life of the people at all levels of ministry.

And he who curses his father or his mother shall surely be put to death. Exodus 21:17

Every one of you shall revere his mother and his father, and keep My Sabbaths: I am the LORD your God. Leviticus 19:3

Cursed is the one who treats his father or his mother with contempt. And all the people shall say, "Amen!" Deuteronomy 27:16

If we reject spiritual mothers and speak against them, we are disobeying God's command. Some who curse the Lord's anointed women will lose their ministries or die prematurely. The word of God consistently calls us to respect fathers and mothers. Those who dishonor their parents bring a curse upon themselves. If we dishonor mothers of the faith and despise the instruction of spiritual mothers it will not go well with us.

Miriam, a Mother in Israel

Then Miriam the prophetess, the sister of Aaron, took the timbrel in her hand; and all the women went out after her with timbrels and with dances. And Miriam answered them: "Sing to the LORD, for He has triumphed gloriously! The horse and its rider He has thrown into the sea!" Exodus 15:20,21

After the Lord triumphed at the Red Sea, Moses sang the prophetic song of the Lord, and Miriam, the anointed prophetess, led the women in a choral response. Miriam used a timbrel to worship as she danced before the Lord. I picture a beautiful scene of men singing a line of prophetic song led by Moses and Miriam leading the women in response. There was great rejoicing in the family of God for His great victory over Egypt. Miriam was a mother in Israel who helped lead the nation in worship. Men certainly recognized the authority of her anointing.

"For I brought you up from the land of Egypt, I redeemed you from the house of bondage; and I sent before you Moses, Aaron, and Miriam" (Micah 6:4). God acknowledged the leadership of Miriam alongside Moses and Aaron. She was a great woman of God who undoubtedly interceded for Moses during his entire life. Miriam was the older sister of Moses who followed the baby in the basket to the place where Pharaoh's daughter bathed (see Exodus 2:4-8; Numbers 26:59). Miriam made arrangements for her mother to be hired to nurse Moses. For eighty years, Miriam prayed for the deliverance of Israel. She was instrumental as an intercessor who travailed for Moses and the nation.

Then Miriam and Aaron spoke against Moses because of the Ethiopian woman whom he had married; for he had married an Ethiopian woman. So they said, "Has the LORD indeed spoken only through Moses? Has He not spoken through us also?" And the LORD heard it. Numbers 12:1,2

The enemy found a weakness in Miriam who influenced her younger brother Aaron in jealousy towards Moses. God's anger released leprosy on Miriam, who was put outside the camp for seven days. Moses' intercession restored her to health. Earlier, Moses' intercession prevented Aaron from premature death at the hands of an angry God.

In the context of Numbers 12, we acknowledge that God did speak to Miriam, the prophetess, through visions, dreams and dark sayings. The Lord acknowledged that she was a prophet but not at the level of Moses who spoke with God face to face. The disease humiliated Miriam and it appears that she fully repented of her jealousies. God restored her in seven days and she never rebelled again.

God paints an accurate picture of the failings of His servants. Moses killed a man in Egypt and disobeyed God's command to speak to the rock. Even though Moses was imperfect, he was a humble anointed prophet of extremely high authority. Miriam had her faults, but God used her as a prophetess and spoke through her to help lead the nation.

Huldah, a Woman with Authority

Now it happened, when the king heard the words of the Book of the Law, that he tore his clothes. Then the king commanded Hilkiah the priest, Ahikam the son of Shaphan, Achbor the son of Michaiah, Shaphan the scribe, and Asaiah a servant of the king, saying, "Go, inquire of the LORD for me, for the people and for all Judah, concerning the words of this book that has been found; for great is the wrath of the LORD that is aroused against us, because our fathers have not obeyed the words of this book, to do according to all that is written concerning us." II Kings 22:11-13

The young reformer King Josiah humbled himself before God during a time of national crisis. He commanded the priest and leaders to seek the Lord for a prophetic word on behalf of the people and all Judah. These men recognized that the anointing was on Huldah, a woman prophetess. Rather than seek out other male prophets or seek the Lord themselves, these men sought the counsel of a pure woman, whom they trusted to deliver the word of the Lord.

So Hilkiah the priest, Ahikam, Achbor, Shaphan, and Asaiah went to Huldah the prophetess, the wife of

Shallum the son of Tikvah, the son of Harhas, keeper of the wardrobe. (She dwelt in Jerusalem in the Second Quarter.) And they spoke with her. Then she said to them, "Thus says the LORD God of Israel, 'Tell the man who sent you to Me, Thus says the LORD: "Behold, I will bring calamity on this place and on its inhabitants— all the words of the book which the king of Judah has read—because they have forsaken Me and burned incense to other gods, that they might provoke Me to anger with all the works of their hands. Therefore My wrath shall be aroused against this place and shall not be quenched." ' " "But to the king of Judah, who sent you to inquire of the LORD, in this manner you shall speak to him, 'Thus says the LORD God of Israel: "Concerning the words which you have heard— because your heart was tender, and you humbled yourself before the LORD when you heard what I spoke against this place and against its inhabitants, that they would become a desolation and a curse, and you tore your clothes and wept before Me, I also have heard you," says the LORD. "Surely, therefore, I will gather you to your fathers, and you shall be gathered to your grave in peace; and your eyes shall not see all the calamity which I will bring on this place." ' " So they brought word to the king.
II Kings 22:14-20

Huldah was a mother in Israel whose voice was heard in a time of national reform. She lived in Jerusalem and was well known to have the word of the Lord. Huldah was a constant intercessor who stood in the gap for the nation. She developed a deep relationship with the Lord and never walked in prophetic flattery or deception.

Josiah called on five men at the highest levels of priesthood and government. All five of these men submitted themselves to the voice of a woman. This is a great model for us today. In a time of reform, the voice of women comes forth.

Many women have been intercessors for decades and their voice is seldom heard. When a pure leader rises up, he is looking for truth and he doesn't care if it comes through a man or a woman. The pure leader wants the sure word of the Lord.

Unfortunately, many men who operate in the prophetic get into mixture. They wander into prophetic flattery, self-promotion and poise their souls over others. Women prophets have to struggle simply to survive. They often remain extremely humble and just keep praying and waiting for their time. Huldah was a godly woman whose time had come.

"Huldah" means "weasel, from its quickness in getting into holes." The name also means "perseverance." Women with the anointing of Huldah have learned to hide prophetic truths deep in their hearts from unrighteous men who would use them and abuse them. They have learned perseverance and relentless intercession. As God reforms the Church, the Huldahs will rise up with the sure word of the Lord. National leaders will be consulting with women they can trust rather than greedy men.

The Law of Jealousy

This is the law of jealousy, when a wife, while under her husband's authority, goes astray and defiles herself, or when the spirit of jealousy comes upon a man, and he becomes jealous of his wife; then he shall stand the woman before the LORD, and the priest shall execute all this law upon her. Then the man shall be free from iniquity, but that woman shall bear her guilt. Numbers 5:29-31

Numbers 5 outlines the "law of jealousy" and provides a test to verify a husband's suspicion if the wife has been unfaithful in the area of marital fidelity. There is no such test in the Law for a man. Historically, it should be obvious that men are at least as unfaithful as women in the area of

43

sexual purity. A cursory observation of American society will lead us to conclude that men and women are at least equally adulterous.

Why is there no adultery test for men listed in the Bible? We mentioned in the last chapter that the Bible often speaks prophetically of men and sons in reference to the Son of God. The passage above is another instance. There is no test for the man because the Son of Man is completely faithful in His pure love towards His beloved bride. The question is whether the bride, made up of both genders of believers, has been faithful to Jesus.

In the adultery test, the priest would scrape biblical curses for adultery into the bitter water and make the woman drink it. If she was guilty, her belly would swell and her thigh would rot. This is a prophetic picture to the Church rather than a gender bias against women. The belly represents the heart of man, the seat of his affections. The word of God is the discerner of the thoughts and intentions of the heart. As a believer drinks the word of God by the Spirit, the living word will bring conviction and a righteous judgment to the inmost being in order to lead a person to repent of his or her adulteries. Understanding the prophetic types throughout scripture will help us in understanding difficult passages like Numbers 5. Let's look at another instance of prophetic typing as it applies to men and women.

Then the LORD spoke to Moses, saying, "Speak to the children of Israel, saying: 'If a woman has conceived, and borne a male child, then she shall be unclean seven days; as in the days of her customary impurity she shall be unclean. And on the eighth day the flesh of his foreskin shall be circumcised. She shall then continue in the blood of her purification thirty-three days. She shall not touch any hallowed thing, nor come into the sanctuary until the days of her purification are fulfilled. But if she bears a female child, then she shall be unclean two weeks, as in

**her customary impurity, and she shall continue in the
blood of her purification sixty-six days. Leviticus 12:1-5**

When the woman birthed a male child, she was unclean
seven days and continued in the blood of her purification for
thirty-three days. When the woman birthed a female child,
she was unclean fourteen days and needed sixty-six days for
purification. A natural interpretation of this and other passages in the Old Testament led to an extremely strong gender bias. God is not biased against women. A baby girl is not
twice as defiling as a baby boy! What is going on here?

The male child is a prophetic picture of Jesus Christ,
born of a woman. He lived thirty-three years to bring purification to the Church of Jesus Christ. He purifies His bride,
pictured in the baby girl, by washing her with the water of
His word found in the sixty-six books of the Bible. God
required the Israelites, under the law, to obey His word to
present prophetic pictures for our instruction. We must study
by the Holy Spirit and recognize the pictures throughout the
entire Bible that are written so that we can be purified and
completely equipped to walk righteously before the Lord.

The Daughters of Zelophehad Received an Inheritance

**Then came the daughters of Zelophehad the son of
Hepher, the son of Gilead, the son of Machir, the son of
Manasseh, from the families of Manasseh the son of
Joseph; and these were the names of his daughters:
Mahlah, Noah, Hoglah, Milcah, and Tirzah. And they
stood before Moses, before Eleazar the priest, and before
the leaders and all the congregation, by the doorway of
the tabernacle of meeting, saying: "Our father died in
the wilderness; but he was not in the company of those
who gathered together against the LORD, in company
with Korah, but he died in his own sin; and he had no
sons. Why should the name of our father be removed**

from among his family because he had no son? Give us a possession among the brothers of our father." So Moses brought their case before the LORD. Numbers 27:1-5

The case of the daughters of Zelophehad established a powerful biblical precedent in the life of Israel, and it prophetically portrays the inheritance women would have as spiritual sons through faith in Christ. These five daughters are mothers in Israel, and we must honor their courage and learn from their example. Moses carefully recorded the details of their genealogy by inspiration of the Holy Spirit. All the names are significant with prophetic meanings that I shall only touch on briefly.

Zelophehad means "first born or first rupture." The daughters of Zelophehad prophetically speak of women birthing into ministry, a rupture of the "men only inheritance club." Five is the number of grace and also speaks of the five-fold ministry. They were descendants of Hepher, which means "well, digging." In order for women to birth into ministry, they have to dig a well into the anointing of the Holy Spirit so that a river flows from their inmost being. Hepher came from Gilead, whose name means "a perpetual fountain, a powerful testimony." This story is a powerful testimony that women have rights to inherit and have authority in the government of the Church.

Gilead was the son of Machir whose name means, "to sell, to betroth, a daughter, to give oneself up" and represents that bride that gives up everything to be betrothed to Jesus as many women are doing. Machir came from Manasseh establishing the daughters of Zelophehehad as descendants of Joseph. Manasseh was the first-born son born to Joseph in Egypt whose name means, "to forget," as Joseph sought to forget the painful past of rejection and captivity. Even so women must be healed of the rejection and captivity of men so they can rule as Joseph did without bitterness. Joseph's name means, "the Lord will add" and he became a great prophet who blessed the nation of Israel and Egypt greatly and saved them from starvation and ruin. Joseph was lifted out of a dungeon into powerful leadership over a nation in a day and prophetically portrays that God will quickly lift anointed prophetic women into places of prominence overnight. Many men will bow down in repentance to receive the blessing God puts on anointed women.

The five daughters' names are also significant. Mahlah means "disease, sickness and pain." Imagine naming your daughter Disease. Noah means "motion, wandering and moving to and fro." Hoglah means "partridge, boxer, the feast has languished." Milcah means "Queen or counsel." Tirzah means "pleasantness, delight and she is willing." Taken as a progression one could picture women coming out of a place where they were considered no better than sickness or disease. Women have been perceived a pain to many men. They have had to go through much wandering and motion, being jerked around by men. Women have the blessing of a partridge and have fought to be accepted. They finally begin to emerge as queens and become a delight to the Lord and man.

The five daughters approached Moses and Eleazor before the door of the tabernacle seeking appropriate judgment for their complaint. They were both determined and respectful. They had carefully prepared their argument and came in perfect agreement to state their cause. They fought for their father's namesake and in effect said that they were qualified to fulfill the responsibilities of inheritance as well as a man would. Moses took it before the Lord in prayer.

And the LORD spoke to Moses, saying: "The daughters of Zelophehad speak what is right; you shall surely give them a possession of inheritance among their father's brothers, and cause the inheritance of their father to pass to them. And you shall speak to the children of Israel, saying: 'If a man dies and has no son,

then you shall cause his inheritance to pass to his daughter.'" Numbers 27:6-8

The Lord told Moses that the daughters of Zelophehad spoke of what was right. We are not given the voice inflection of the Lord, but the response of the Lord is extremely strong and directive. The laws of inheritance until that time passed all rights down from fathers to first-born sons. This was a prophetic picture of Father God giving all the inheritance to His first-born, the Lord Jesus Christ.

In the story of the daughters of Zelophehad, we observe the Lord commanding Moses to edit the law so as to include daughters when there are no sons. This is a prophetic picture that daughters will one day be included in sonship rights through faith in Christ Jesus. The daughters of Zelophehad were given full inheritance status and by implication, they had a voice among the elders of their clan.

The book of Numbers closes with final instructions that the daughters of Zelophehad were to marry within their tribe so that the inheritance of land would stay associated with their father's tribe. They were more than willing to submit to this instruction (see Numbers 36:1-13). The anointing on women to lead in the Church is to be used to govern and equip the Church, not for personal gain or selfish reasons.

The five daughters in this story were not rebellious but righteous in their submission to leaders. They were not doormats. They rightfully brought their rights before Moses and received the inheritance of their father. There is a need for women to stand up for their rights in Christ before Church leaders and at the same time be submissive to men in leadership. The body of Christ will grow to a place where men realize that it is right for women to have inheritance rights in the leadership of the Church. The story concludes the book of Numbers, which points to the end of the age. God knew that women would not be included in leadership until the end of the Church age, at the dawn of the third day.

Queen Esther, a Woman with International Authority

Now it happened on the third day that Esther put on her royal robes and stood in the inner court of the king's palace, across from the king's house, while the king sat on his royal throne in the royal house, facing the entrance of the house. So it was, when the king saw Queen Esther standing in the court, that she found favor in his sight, and the king held out to Esther the golden scepter that was in his hand. Then Esther went near and touched the top of the scepter. And the king said to her, "What do you wish, Queen Esther? What is your request? It shall be given to you—up to half the kingdom!" Esther 5:1-3

Queen Esther was an historical woman who rose to a place of international authority. Esther fasted and prayed to seek the Lord's favor before breaching protocol to enter the king's audience without an invitation. The Esther fast was to prevail upon the king to take up arms against the conspiracy of Haman to exterminate the Jews in the kingdom.

It happened on the "third day" that Esther put on her royal robes and came into the throne room before the king to make her petition. There are tremendous prophetic pictures in the book of Esther of the third-day Church putting on her royal robes and having great favor with the King of Kings in intercession. The Lord Himself will extend the scepter to a Church that has purified herself and prepared herself to go into the king's presence.

Queen Esther is also a prophetic picture of the favor God will give women in the last days. Many women have been intercessors who have prayed and fasted for their children, the Church and their regions. Although, many intercessors are not highly visible in the Church, their authority comes from being visible in the throne room of the Most High God.

The relationship between the female Esther and the male

Mordecai demonstrates a beautiful partnership between men and women that is necessary to overcome evil in the last days. The Lord established both of them in positions of national and international authority. In the book of Esther, the queen has the higher authority.

Men have had the higher authority in the Church for nearly 2,000 years and the corruption overall in the Church through history has been legendary. God is going to purge His Church with fire and cleanse her from the works of "man's hands." God will establish the leadership of the body of Christ with those believers who qualify with clean hearts and pure hands. His apostolic government will be those who are first of all devoted to prayer. Second, they will be devoted to the ministry of the word as taught by the Holy Spirit (Acts 6:4).

Presently, we have a huge imbalance in the ratio of women intercessors to men. In the church where we minister it us usually 8 to 1, and I am often the "1" male in the midst. I've talked with other men who intercede and this is a common observation. Intercessors who behold Jesus with unveiled face are gradually transformed to become like Him (II Corinthians 3:18). Our faces are unveiled to behold Him as we persevere in worship, praise and prayer over extended seasons. God releases revelation to those who press in to know Him intimately.

Women are characteristically more wired for intimacy in relationships while men are generally more wired for accomplishing goals and completing tasks. We need both in the body of Christ, but men cannot neglect an intimate relationship with Jesus in order to perform tasks in the house of God. Performance orientation leads to the works of man's hands that are independent of the anointing power of the Holy Spirit. Man's works produce a religious house that is not built by God and is a labor in vain. Obviously, both men and women can labor in vain when they operate independent of the Holy Spirit.

The relational aspect of women in pursuit of intimacy with God is a virtue men need to learn from in the last days. God releases pure prophetic words to those who walk in intimacy. We need the prophets who pray, pray and pray. Many of them will be women. The apostles must also be devoted to prayer and the strategic development of God's house. They may be more task oriented than prophets, but they must learn to walk in a pure relationship with the Holy Spirit to be effective in building God's pure house.

God calls us to honor the anointing on fathers and mothers. There is a perfect balance the Spirit wants to bring us to in the last days. As we move into this balance and as the anointings of men and women blend together, the power released will enable us to grow in dominion over areas we've never been able to conquer before. As a result of this pure unity of the Spirit in submission to the anointing on leaders in the body, whether male or female, we will walk in the works that Jesus walked in and even greater works (John 14:12-14). The greatest days of Church history are just ahead as Deborahs awake and begin to sing, along with Baraks, the anointed song of ministry the Lord gives them.

The Wise Woman from Abel

And he went through all the tribes of Israel to Abel and Beth Maachah and all the Berites. So they were gathered together and also went after Sheba. Then they came and besieged him in Abel of Beth Maachah; and they cast up a siege mound against the city, and it stood by the rampart. And all the people who were with Joab battered the wall to throw it down. Then a wise woman cried out from the city, "Hear, hear! Please say to Joab, 'Come nearby, that I may speak with you.'" When he had come near to her, the woman said, "Are you Joab?" He

51

answered, "I am." Then she said to him, "Hear the words of your maidservant." And he answered, "I am listening."

So she spoke, saying, "They used to talk in former times, saying, 'They shall surely seek guidance at Abel,' and so they would end disputes. I am among the peaceable and faithful in Israel. You seek to destroy a city and <u>a mother in Israel</u>. Why would you swallow up the inheritance of the LORD?"

And Joab answered and said, "Far be it, far be it from me, that I should swallow up or destroy! That is not so. But a man from the mountains of Ephraim, Sheba the son of Bichri by name, has raised his hand against the king, against David. Deliver him only, and I will depart from the city."

So the woman said to Joab, "Watch, his head will be thrown to you over the wall." Then the woman in her wisdom went to all the people. And they cut off the head of Sheba the son of Bichri, and threw it out to Joab. Then he blew a trumpet, and they withdrew from the city, every man to his tent. So Joab returned to the king at Jerusalem. II Samuel 20:14-22 (underlining mine)

This unnamed woman from the city of Abel was a mother in Israel. Her courageous intercession saved an entire city from certain destruction. She operated in godly wisdom and people listened to her counsel. Joab declared, "I am listening." He showed honor to a mother in Israel and gave her time to talk to the people and produce Sheba's head.

This virtuous woman was faithful to God and sought to live in peace. She recognized that Sheba was a rebellious man plotting against the Lord's anointed king. Allowing Sheba to remain in the city would have caused the death of the city. She refused to give refuge to the rebellion of Sheba and had his head cut off and thrown over the wall.

Churches too often tolerate the rebellious spirit of Sheba

in their midst. Intercessors can cut the head off that devil in the spiritual realm. If necessary, after following biblical guidelines, a divisive person should be asked to leave the fellowship if he will not repent. There are Sheba spirits that empower dissention, divisions, offenses and rebellions against the Sr. Pastor. Those evil spirits can destroy the move of God in an entire city. God may have chosen you to be the intercessor that stands in the gap for your city and lead you to throw Sheba's head over your city wall.

Simeon and Anna

Then Simeon blessed them, and said to Mary His mother, "Behold, this Child is destined for the fall and rising of many in Israel, and for a sign which will be spoken against (yes, a sword will pierce through your own soul also), that the thoughts of many hearts may be revealed."

Now there was one, Anna, a prophetess, the daughter of Phanuel, of the tribe of Asher. She was of a great age, and had lived with a husband seven years from her virginity; and this woman was a widow of about eighty-four years, who did not depart from the temple, but served God with fastings and prayers night and day. And coming in that instant she gave thanks to the Lord, and spoke of Him to all those who looked for redemption in Jerusalem. Luke 2:34-38

The elders Simeon and Anna, in the temple of God, both rejoiced to see the birth of Jesus, their Messiah. Simeon and Anna are a beautiful picture of men and women working together in the house of God to birth last-day moves of the Spirit. For our purposes, we will look closer at Anna, another mother of the faith.

Luke recognized that Anna was an anointed prophetess who spoke of Jesus to all those who looked for redemption in

Jerusalem. Anna spent about sixty years serving God with fastings and prayers night and day. When she saw the baby Jesus, by the Holy Spirit, Anna recognized Him as the Christ and gave thanks to the Lord. She began speaking of Him to all who came to the temple area in Jerusalem. Did the Jewish pilgrims listen to Anna? Did men allow her to teach them about the Redeemer of Israel? Of course they did!

Imagine the anointing on this woman who never left the presence of God for sixty years. She fasted, prayed, worshipped and served God devotedly with all her heart. She was married only seven years and then widowed. Anna, whose name means grace, gave herself completely to God who became her true husband. Anna would have studied the scriptures and engaged with the other saints who worshipped and looked for the Messiah to come. It would have been foolish for a man to reject Anna's teaching simply because she was a woman. There is no indication that Anna was prohibited from teaching or prophesying in God's temple.

Anna was the daughter of Phanuel, which means "vision of God" and is the Greek rendering of Peniel meaning "the face of God" from the root word meaning "to behold; to turn to God." Anna turned her eyes to her heavenly Father and beheld His face. By beholding Him, she became full of His grace and truth. Anna is a picture of anointed women prophets and the Church in the days before Jesus' second coming.

Anna was of the tribe of Asher. The New Testament rarely tells us what tribe a person is from. When it does, it is always a prophetic picture or fulfillment of prophecy. Asher means, "fortunate, happy, blessed." Asher was the eighth born son of Jacob, which points to new beginnings. The gate of Asher was the 11th gate on the western wall of Ezekiel's vision of the New Jerusalem (Ezekiel 48:30-35). West speaks to us of the setting sun and the end of the age.

The gate of Asher represents entering into the blessings of God through faith in the virtue of Christ's atoning work.

This includes salvation, healing, total wellness and great prosperity. **"Bread from Asher shall be rich, and he shall yield royal dainties" (Genesis 49:20).** The bread of Asher is rich revelation food that equips spiritual kings to reign and rule with Christ. This kind of rich revelation of the Bread of Life comes to those who pursue the Lord as Anna did. God released powerful revelation to Anna and wants to give this revelation to women and men who will diligently seek Him.

And of Asher he said: "Asher is most blessed of sons; let him be favored by his brothers, and let him dip his foot in oil. Your sandals shall be iron and bronze; as your days, so shall your strength be. "There is no one like the God of Jeshurun, who rides the heavens to help you, and in His excellency on the clouds. The eternal God is your refuge, and underneath are the everlasting arms; He will thrust out the enemy from before you, and will say, 'Destroy!' Then Israel shall dwell in safety, the fountain of Jacob alone, in a land of grain and new wine; His Heavens shall also drop dew. Happy are you, O Israel! Who is like you, a people saved by the LORD, the shield of your help and the sword of your majesty! Your enemies shall submit to you, and you shall tread down their high places." Deuteronomy 33:24-29

Moses prophesied that Asher would be the most blessed of sons, with his foot dipped in oil wearing sandals of bronze with long life and great strength. The King of Kings will ride on the clouds to help Asher. This is a picture of the Lord Jesus Christ coming to save Israel and His Church in the last days. Asher pictures the Church that walks in authority and power to judge the nations. Asher's blessings include an incredible transfer of wealth from the wicked to the righteous in order to fund extraordinary last-day revival crusades and equipping throughout the earth. Isaiah prophesied about this wealth transfer.

Her gain and her pay will be set apart for the LORD;

it will not be treasured nor laid up, for her gain will be <u>for those who dwell before the LORD</u>, to eat sufficiently, and for fine clothing. Isaiah 23:18 (underlining mine)

Anna was from Asher and dwelt before the Lord. The wealth of the wicked of the end days will be set apart for the Lord and will be given to those Annas who can be trusted to steward the money according to the leading of the Holy Spirit. Many Annas will be faithful intercessors who were married to business tycoons who die because they do not repent or fear God. All of their wealth is transferred to the faithful wife who then uses the money for the kingdom of God. This is already happening in America and a great amount of wealth is in the hands of women already.

The tribe of Asher lived on the seacoast, which speaks to us of a vision for the nations. Anna was of this tribe. Prophetically she represents the last-day Church that is blessed with the bread of life and takes the word of God to the nations. Having lived on a shoe string budget for many years in missions, I long for the days of Asher where we can fully fund mission's trips, materials, equipment and supplies to reap a last-day harvest. This great wealth transfer will come as we become corporate Annas fasting, praying, serving God day and night in the temple and beholding the grace of Jesus.

For you know the grace of our Lord Jesus Christ, that though He was rich, yet for your sakes He became poor, that you through His poverty might become rich. II Corinthians 8:9

There is a virtue in the poverty of Jesus on the cross that enables us to be blessed with the wealth to accomplish all that God calls us to do. We must behold Jesus to know His grace. Beholding by the Spirit comes as we become like Anna. As we grow in faith in His virtue, the Holy Spirit will release words of wisdom, and His favor will be upon us to obtain the wealth. It will be given to those who dwell before the presence of the Lord. It will be given to Annas. Do not despise your mothers of faith, but rather learn from them and submit to the anointing on them as it applies to you. God promises to bless us as we honor our mothers and fathers.

CHAPTER 3

WOMEN ARE SONS OF GOD THROUGH FAITH

For you are all sons of God through faith in Christ Jesus. For as many of you as were baptized into Christ have put on Christ. There is neither Jew nor Greek, there is neither slave nor free, there is neither male nor female; for you are all one in Christ Jesus. And if you are Christ's, then you are Abraham's seed, and heirs according to the promise. Galatians 3:26-29

We have learned that God created "man" in the image of God, male and female He created them. God created "them" to exercise dominion on Earth, in loving righteous agreement, under the anointing of the Holy Spirit. God's fifth commandment included honoring spiritual mothers and is the only old covenant commandment with a promise of blessing. We have also seen the principle that the natural comes first and then the spiritual.

The Old Testament is heavily focused on natural Israel and has a prophetic bent towards men representing the Son of God and women representing the Church. The heavy emphasis on male leadership in the Old Testament points to the headship of the Son of Man, Christ Jesus. God gave us several prophetic pictures of women in places of leadership in the Old Testament such as Miriam, Deborah, Huldah and Esther.

Now we want to examine the change that occurred in New Testament theology concerning women in leadership positions of the Church. The key principle in the New Testament is that there is no gender bias regarding sonship rights. In the Old Testament, a person had to be a male in order to inherit sonship rights except in the rare case noted in the daughters of Zelophehad.

Paul accurately taught the new covenant theology that a person qualified to be a son of God through faith in Christ Jesus. Qualifications for sonship were not based on being a Jew or a Greek. This was a radical revelation to Peter and the early apostles as we have noted earlier. Qualifications for sonship rights were not based on being slave or free. A person's economic status has nothing to do with their position as a son of God.

Finally, Paul recognized that sonship rights were not based on being male or female. **There is no gender qualification for being recognized as a "son of God."** The only qualification for being an adopted son of God is faith in Christ Jesus. This is completely consistent in the application of spiritual benefits. Paul recognized that gender barriers were broken down in Christ when he said, **"there is neither male nor female" (Galatians 3:28).**

Peter recognized that God was no respecter of persons and that God's love provided salvation for all who believed on the Lord Jesus Christ (Acts 10:34,35, John 3:16). The bride of Christ is made up of women and men who believe in their Heavenly Bridegroom (Revelation 21:2,9). The body of Christ is composed of both genders who believe (I Corinthians 12:27). The temple of God, built by living stones, is made up of males and females who put their trust in Jesus (I Corinthians 3:16; Ephesians 2:20-22). There is absolutely no gender bias in the heart of God towards women as His adopted sons.

The Anointing Falls on Men and Women

And it shall come to pass afterward that I will pour out My Spirit on all flesh; your sons and your daughters shall prophesy, your old men shall dream dreams, your young men shall see visions. And also on My menservants and on My maidservants I will pour out My Spirit in those days. Joel 2:28-29

Joel prophesied that the anointing would fall on men and women, sons and daughters, menservants and maidservants. The anointing is an endowment of power of the Holy Spirit to enable a believer to bear fruit for the glory of God. The anointing evidences the call of God to perform ministry.

Joel notes that "your daughters shall prophesy." A great portion of the Church does not believe in New Testament prophesying or prophets. That won't stop God from pouring out His Spirit on women who will speak as the mouthpiece of God. If a woman speaks the word of the Lord, under the anointing, God is going to judge men and women for their response to that word as if God Himself was speaking it. At certain times, men will need to submit to the word of the Lord on women, as they did to Deborah and Huldah, if they are to completely follow the Holy Spirit.

Men who reject women prophets are in danger of rejecting God. Prophets and apostles are the two founding office leaders in the development of the Church. **"Now, therefore, you are no longer strangers and foreigners, but fellow citizens with the saints and members of the household of God, having been built on the foundation of the apostles**

and prophets, Jesus Christ Himself being the chief cornerstone, in whom the whole building, being joined together, grows into a holy temple in the Lord, in whom you also are being built together for a dwelling place of God in the Spirit." Ephesians 2:19-22

God is anointing women prophets today as He has throughout history. We must learn to know men and women by the Spirit of God so that we can choose to submit to the anointing on them. As we submit to the anointing, we are submitting to Christ who anointed them.

On the next day we who were Paul's companions departed and came to Caesarea, and entered the house of Philip the evangelist, who was one of the seven, and stayed with him. Now this man had four virgin daughters who prophesied. Acts 21:8-9

The Holy Spirit wanted us to know that Philip had four pure daughters who prophesied. This is a revelation of New Testament Church truth. The first fruit outpouring of Joel's prophecy was partially fulfilled as women prophesied. Philip's daughters were recognized as having a prophetic ministry. Perhaps some of them were recognized as office level prophets.

God's anointing has no gender bias. Jesus said that we must abide in Him and that apart from Him, we could do nothing to bear fruit (John 15:1-5). Abiding in Jesus requires that we abide in the anointing of the Holy Spirit who enables us to do every good and pleasing work of the Father. Women as well as men can learn to abide in Christ and His anointing. Faithful women can bear fruit for the glory of God just as faithful men can.

We do not see any gender bias in the salvation of souls, sonship rights, the bride of Christ, the body of Christ, the temple of God or the anointing. Is it possible that there is no gender bias in God's word related to women in Church government? Yes of course! God is completely consistent. He is

no respecter of persons. He still wants "them" to rule in righteous agreement in the house of God with Jesus as the head.

Church government offices are to be held by those
whom God calls and anoints for these positions. We have
seen clear scriptural proof that God pours out His Spirit, His
anointing, on both men and women. In areas of Church government, God does not suddenly become gender biased in
the release of His anointing. All women of faith are sons of
God and if God calls and anoints them to leadership, they
qualify based on God's anointing not gender.

**Now you are the body of Christ, and members indi-
vidually. And God has appointed these in the church:
first apostles, second prophets, third teachers, after that
miracles, then gifts of healings, helps, administrations,
varieties of tongues. I Corinthians 12:27,28**

**And He Himself gave some to be apostles, some
prophets, some evangelists, and some pastors and teachers, for the equipping of the saints for the work of ministry, for the edifying of the body of Christ, till we all
come to the unity of the faith and of the knowledge of the
Son of God, to a perfect man, to the measure of the
stature of the fullness of Christ; that we should no longer
be children, tossed to and fro and carried about with
every wind of doctrine, by the trickery of men, in the
cunning craftiness of deceitful plotting, but, speaking the
truth in love, may grow up in all things into Him who is
the head—Christ—from whom the whole body, joined
and knit together by what every joint supplies, according
to the effective working by which every part does its
share, causes growth of the body for the edifying of itself
in love. Ephesians 4:11-16**

God gives the Church apostles, prophets, evangelists,
pastors and teachers to equip the saints for the work of ministry, to edify the body, to bring the body to unity, knowledge
and the fullness of maturity. The Bible says that these office

gifts are given to enable us to become **"a perfect man."** Isn't the body also the bride of Christ? Is God saying that only men can be part of the body here? Of course not! He is teaching the principle that the body is a picture of the body of the Son of God made up of "sons of God." Does that mean that all five-fold ministers must be men? No!

God is not a respecter of persons. He anoints those who respond in faith and obedience to the Holy Spirit. A believer must qualify to become a leader in the house of God through faithful obedience and equipping by the Holy Spirit.

The original apostles devoted themselves to prayer and the ministry of the word. They established a pattern of Church governmental leadership that those set apart by God to lead must be devoted to a lifestyle of worship, praise, prayer and intercession along with diligent study and ministry of the word of God.

All of Jesus' original apostles were men, just as all of the heads of the twelve tribes of Israel were men. Does this exclude women from being apostles and prophets? No! Jesus came during a transitional time period in the kingdom of God. He transitioned from natural Israel to spiritual Israel, the Church. Jesus lived His natural life under the Old Covenant and fulfilled all the law. The Church was not birthed until after Jesus ascended on high.

Under the Old Covenant, all the priests of Levi and all Rabbis were men. Again this points to the true High Priest, the Son of Man. Jesus chose only twelve men as part of fulfilling the Law, but He transitioned from the Law and prophetically revealed the change as He appeared to women first after His resurrection (see Matthew 28:9,10).

Sons are led by the Spirit

For if you live according to the flesh you will die; but if by the Spirit you put to death the deeds of the body,

you will live. For as many as are led by the Spirit of God, these are sons of God. Romans 8:13-14

Sons of God are led by the Spirit Who enables them to put to death the deeds of the body in order to have life. True sons of God do not live according to the flesh. This applies to both men and women in the body of Christ. In order to qualify for a last-day governmental position in the body of Christ, an individual must become a mature son. Again, this is not a gender bias, but it is a standard of maturity. Mature sons have allowed the Spirit to crucify their flesh and have grown in Christ-like character. They operate by the Spirit at all times, and this enables them to lead in the house of God.

Now I say that the heir, as long as he is a child, does not differ at all from a slave, though he is master of all, but is under guardians and stewards until the time appointed by the father. Even so we, when we were children, were in bondage under the elements of the world. But when the fullness of the time had come, God sent forth His Son, born of a woman, born under the law, to redeem those who were under the law, that we might receive the adoption as sons. And because you are sons, God has sent forth the Spirit of His Son into your hearts, crying out, "Abba, Father!" Therefore you are no longer a slave but a son, and if a son, then an heir of God through Christ. Galatians 4:1-7

We are heirs of Christ and have an extraordinary inheritance through faith. We do not access that inheritance if we are immature and walk by the flesh. As long as we are immature, according to Paul, we are no different from a slave even though by position we have sonship rights as master of all. The Lord Himself keeps us under guardians and tutors until we mature. He will not release the fullness of our inheritance, including true anointing as a five-fold minister of God, while we remain immature and act according to the flesh. One may be called to be an apostle but not chosen yet because of immaturity.

Mature sons learn to walk by the Spirit in all things. They learn the Good Shepherd's voice and will not follow a stranger. Mature sons don't need the Law to tutor them or intense accountability structures because they love God with all their hearts and have grown to willingly follow the law of the Spirit of life in Christ Jesus within them at all times.

Walk in the Spirit

I say then: Walk in the Spirit, and you shall not fulfill the lust of the flesh. Galatians 5:16 And those who are Christ's have crucified the flesh with its passions and desires. If we live in the Spirit, let us also walk in the Spirit. Galatians 5:24,25

Paul's main message in Galatians is to walk in the Spirit. There is no power in religion or Church traditions to overcome the lust of the flesh. Those who walk by the Spirit will put to death the deeds of the flesh and will be conformed to the image of God's Son. Those who mature in faith may be called and commissioned as five-fold office level leaders in the body of Christ. They will not all be "pastors." They will be apostles, prophets, evangelists and teachers as well. Our present Church structure is inadequate to recognize the diversities of the five-fold calling so that we usually call every minister "pastor."

God has anointed me as a five-fold teacher in the body of Christ, and I serve full time in a local church. The people call me Pastor Scott. By God's grace, I have a pastor's heart to some degree, but I do not have that specific anointing nearly as strong as the call as a teacher. The Lord spoke to me that I was anointed as a teacher in the body of Christ and He has confirmed that calling many times. While I may have other office callings, I must wait on God to establish me. This is true for every servant of God, whether male or female.

Many women have learned to pray, fast and obey the Holy Spirit's leadings. They have studied the word of God and devoted themselves to God and serving people in the love of Christ. Many of those women who mature in walking by the Spirit are qualifying as mature sons to walk in the inheritance of God. The inheritance includes walking in the fullness of the anointing God ordained for them to walk in. This will include healing the sick, casting out demons, teaching with authority and providing governmental leadership in the body of Christ. God is no respecter of persons. He does not qualify His leaders based on gender. God qualifies leaders based on His calling and the person's consistent obedience in response.

The Lord will take His last-day, five-fold ministers through many trials to burn the flesh out of them before they qualify to be truly anointed as His leaders. What we see in the Church today is not necessarily the order that God established. Many "pastors" are ordained by man and not by God. Many don't have power over their own flesh, let alone a tormented, demonized person.

The eyes of God are looking throughout the earth for those He is calling to lead His people faithfully. Many are called but few are chosen (Matthew 20:16). While many men are leading churches with programmed religion, many women have been faithfully praying, seeking God and waiting upon the Lord for His anointing. All true promotion in the things of the Spirit comes from God. The Lord is going to promote faithful women to positions of leadership because they have become mature sons who walk by the Spirit. Men in churches had better learn to submit to the anointing and walk in the Spirit or they may find themselves outside of God's leadership when He reforms His house. Carnal leaders, be they male or female, will not stand as

God's ministers in the last days. Only those who mature in faith, walking by the Spirit in righteousness, holiness, love and truth will stand and lead on that day. I have no doubt that many anointed women will be there.

CHAPTER 4

CHRIST AND WOMEN

But when the fullness of the time had come, God sent forth His Son, born of a woman, born under the law. Galatians 4:4

Jesus Christ humbled Himself when He left His glorious throne in heaven and came to Earth. Jesus honored Mary and women by being formed in her womb. Jesus was born of a woman. This is a great testimony of God's favor on women. God entrusted His own Son to be carried, nurtured, breast fed, loved, taught and raised by a woman along with her righteous husband Joseph.

Now in the sixth month the angel Gabriel was sent by God to a city of Galilee named Nazareth, to a virgin betrothed to a man whose name was Joseph, of the house of David. The virgin's name was Mary. And having come in, the angel said to her, "Rejoice, highly favored one, the Lord is with you; blessed are you among women!" But when she saw him, she was troubled at his saying, and considered what manner of greeting this was. Then the angel said to her, "Do not be afraid, Mary, for you have

found favor with God. And behold, you will conceive in your womb and bring forth a Son, and shall call His name JESUS. He will be great, and will be called the Son of the Highest; and the Lord God will give Him the throne of His father David. And He will reign over the house of Jacob forever, and of His kingdom there will be no end." Then Mary said to the angel, "How can this be, since I do not know a man?" And the angel answered and said to her, "The Holy Spirit will come upon you, and the power of the Highest will overshadow you; there-fore, also, that Holy One who is to be born will be called the Son of God. Now indeed, Elizabeth your relative has also conceived a son in her old age; and this is now the sixth month for her who was called barren. For with God nothing will be impossible." Then Mary said, "Behold the maidservant of the Lord! Let it be to me according to your word." And the angel departed from her. Luke 1:26-38

Mary was highly favored by God. Oh, what a great blessing to have the favor of God! God wants to pour out His favor on many women who will allow the Holy Spirit to plant the seed of Christ in their hearts by the word of God. The Lord is still bringing forth moves of His Spirit by inter-cessors who pray and seek His face. Mary was chosen by God to bring forth Jesus into the world. Overwhelmed with emotion and anointed by the Spirit, Mary gave thanks to God.

And Mary said: "My soul magnifies the Lord, and my spirit has rejoiced in God my Savior. For He has regarded the lowly state of His maidservant; for behold, henceforth all generations will call me blessed. For He who is mighty has done great things for me, and holy is His name. And His mercy is on those who fear Him from generation to generation. He has shown strength with His arm; He has scattered the proud in the imagination of their hearts. He has put down the mighty from their thrones, and exalted the lowly. He has filled the hungry with good things, and the rich He has sent away empty. He has helped His servant Israel, in remembrance of His mercy, as He spoke to our fathers, to Abraham and to his seed forever." Luke 1:46-55

Mary certainly had an intimate walk with God. She was a humble handmaiden willing to do whatever the Lord asked of her. God opposes the proud but flows His grace to the humble. Mary was humble and received extraordinary grace. What an example to us all. God will flow His grace to humble believing women and use them far beyond their greatest expectations.

Jesus Submitted to His Mother

So when they saw Him, they were amazed; and His mother said to Him, "Son, why have You done this to us? Look, Your father and I have sought You anxiously." And He said to them, "Why did you seek Me? Did you not know that I must be about My Father's business?" But they did not understand the statement which He spoke to them. Then He went down with them and came to Nazareth, and was subject to them, but His mother kept all these things in her heart. And Jesus increased in wisdom and stature, and in favor with God and men. Luke 2:48-52

While Jesus was growing up, He fulfilled the law by honoring His father and His mother. Jesus **"was <u>subject</u> to them."** The Greek word "hupotasso" is used here and is found a total of forty times in the New Testament. Hupotasso means "to be in submission, be subject to, to obey, to be under obedience." Jesus clearly chose to submit to a woman during His maturing years. He honored Mary and cared for her throughout His life.

Jesus was called to be about His Father's business, but He remained subject to His parents until God called Him out as a man at the proper time. There are little boys in Church today who will be great leaders in the body of Christ. God will call them to submit to their parents and learn from women in the Church. Henrietta Mears provided some inspirational teaching and guidance to young Billy Graham at Forest Home Conference Center long before Billy became the best known evangelist of our era.

Henrietta Mears also led Bill and Vonnette Bright to faith in Jesus. Bill Bright received instruction from a woman and went on to found Campus Crusade for Christ International. God used a woman from Campus Crusade to help lead me to place my faith in Jesus in 1974. When a woman has the words of life, it is wise to submit to her teaching.

Jesus' First Miracle

On the third day there was a wedding in Cana of Galilee, and the mother of Jesus was there. Now both Jesus and His disciples were invited to the wedding. And when they ran out of wine, the mother of Jesus said to Him, "They have no wine." Jesus said to her, "Woman, what does your concern have to do with Me? My hour has not yet come." His mother said to the servants, "Whatever He says to you, do it." John 2:1-5

Jesus' first miracle recorded in John's gospel was prompted by the influence of His mother. Jesus called her "woman" which indicates that He was no longer subject to her in parental authority. Mary believed that Jesus could miraculously solve the problem and rescue the wedding from embarrassment. Jesus honored her request and changed the water into wine. Jesus chose to submit to Mary for many years and allowed women to minister to Him during His ministry. We should follow His example.

A wonderful story is told of an anointed leader in the Charismatic renewal who was trying to bring the anointing of the Holy Spirit to Catholic leaders in Rome. When asked point blank what he believed about Mary, the Charismatic leader replied something like, "I'm more of a believer in Mary than you are! Mary told us to listen to Jesus and do whatever He says to do. I believe Mary's words and I do whatever Jesus tells me to do!" That satisfied the Catholics and they listened to the man testify about the moving of the Holy Spirit.

The Samaritan Woman

A woman of Samaria came to draw water. Jesus said to her, "Give Me a drink." For His disciples had gone away into the city to buy food. Then the woman of Samaria said to Him, "How is it that You, being a Jew, ask a drink from me, a Samaritan woman?" For Jews have no dealings with Samaritans. Jesus answered and said to her, "If you knew the gift of God, and who it is who says to you, 'Give Me a drink,' you would have asked Him, and He would have given you living water." The woman said to Him, "Sir, You have nothing to draw with, and the well is deep. Where then do You get that living water? Are You greater than our father Jacob, who gave us the well, and drank from it himself, as well as his sons and his livestock?" Jesus answered and said to her, "Whoever drinks of this water will thirst again, but whoever drinks of the water that I shall give him will never thirst. But the water that I shall give him will become in him a fountain of water springing up into everlasting life." The woman said to Him, "Sir, give me this water, that I may not thirst, nor come here to draw."

Jesus said to her, "Go, call your husband, and come here." The woman answered and said, "I have no husband." Jesus said to her, "You have well said, 'I have no husband,' "for you have had five husbands, and the one whom you now have is not your husband; in that you spoke truly." The woman said to Him, "Sir, I perceive that You are a prophet. Our fathers worshipped on this mountain, and you Jews say that in Jerusalem is the place where one ought to worship." Jesus said to her, "Woman, believe Me, the hour is coming when you will neither on this mountain, nor in Jerusalem, worship the Father. You worship what you do not know; we know what we worship, for salvation is of the Jews. But the hour is coming, and now is, when the true worshipers will worship the Father in spirit and truth; for the Father is seeking such to worship Him. God is Spirit, and those who worship Him must worship in spirit and truth." The woman said to Him, "I know that Messiah is coming" (who is called Christ). "When He comes, He will tell us all things." Jesus said to her, "I who speak to you am He." John 4:7-26

The longest conversation recorded with Jesus and another person was His talk with the Samaritan woman at the well. A normal Jewish rabbi would never be caught speaking to a woman alone in public and he would never associate with an unclean Samaritan. Jesus had no religious traditions binding Him. He only operated by the leading of the Holy Spirit. Jesus revealed a glorious teaching to this Samaritan woman and revealed Himself to her as the Messiah.

Jesus asked the woman for a drink from the well. In that, He humbled Himself to receive from the woman what she could give to Him. He had the power to bring the water up out of the well and into His mouth, but He chose to seek help from a woman. This woman appears to have had a most sordid past in relationship to men and Jesus knew it. This was no barrier to Him revealing the Father's heart that was seeking true worshipers. Her fallen condition did not prohibit her from conversing with the King of Kings.

This unique woman was transformed by her encounter with Jesus and raced to the town with evangelistic fervor. Even though she was known as a woman of ill repute, the townspeople listened to her testimony and came out to see Jesus for themselves.

In the meantime His disciples urged Him, saying, "Rabbi, eat." But He said to them, "I have food to eat of which you do not know." Therefore the disciples said to one another, "Has anyone brought Him anything to eat?" Jesus said to them, "My food is to do the will of Him who sent Me, and to finish His work. Do you not say, 'There are still four months and then comes the harvest'? Behold, I say to you, lift up your eyes and look at the fields, for they are already white for harvest!" John 4:31-35

Jesus' belly was filled with compassion for lost people. The food that satisfied Him was to bring in a harvest of souls for His Father. The Holy Spirit gave Jesus a grace to fast and a focus on winning a town. The Holy Spirit led Jesus to use a sinful woman as a means to reach the harvest. The most effective evangelists are often those who have just recently been touched by Jesus. They have a lot of unsaved friends and they have a testimony. Jesus doesn't wait until a new convert has every area of their life together before He uses them. This woman didn't have a Bible College degree, but she had a powerful encounter with Jesus. God used her greatly to reach a harvest.

Jesus exhorted His disciples to lift up their eyes and see the harvest. They were focused on getting a nice lunch together and resting by the well. At that moment, the Samaritans were flocking to the well of salvation for a drink of living water. There was no time to eat and Jesus knew it. The woman brought a whole village to Jesus, the Bread of Life.

Women Supported Jesus Financially

Now it came to pass, afterward, that He went through every city and village, preaching and bringing the glad tidings of the kingdom of God. And the twelve were with Him, and certain women who had been healed of evil spirits and infirmities—Mary called Magdalene, out of whom had come seven demons, and Joanna the wife of Chuza, Herod's steward, and Susanna, and many others who provided for Him from their substance. Luke 8:1-3

Certain women joined the twelve in following Jesus. Jesus healed them and in gratitude they became His followers. Among them was Mary Magdalene, a redeemed woman that few churches would welcome today. Joanna's husband worked for the evil ruler Herod but that did not bother Jesus either. Women followed Jesus and provided for Him from their money. There is no place in the New Testament that indicates that men gave money to Jesus' ministry. We can assume that some men did support Jesus, but the scriptures point out the gifts of the women, not the men.

Judas Iscariot had the moneybag and stole from it. He was the team treasurer and did a lousy job to say the least. Thousands of people were healed by Jesus including ten lepers. Only one of them turned back to give thanks. Not everyone healed by Jesus showed gratitude or gave to support His ministry. The Holy Spirit wanted us to know the names of certain women who responded in great gratitude. Mary, Joanna and Susanna gave to provide for Jesus out of their substance. Jesus received it with thankfulness and used it to fund His ministry.

Jesus Prayed and Laid Hands on Women

Now He was teaching in one of the synagogues on the Sabbath. And behold, there was a woman who had a spirit of infirmity eighteen years, and was bent over and could in no way raise herself up. But when Jesus saw her, He called her to Him and said to her, "Woman, you are loosed from your infirmity." And He laid His hands on her, and immediately she was made straight, and glorified God. But the ruler of the synagogue answered with indignation, because Jesus had healed on the Sabbath; and he said to the crowd, "There are six days on which men ought to work; therefore come and be healed on them, and not on the Sabbath day." The Lord then answered him and said, "Hypocrite! Does not each one of you on the Sabbath loose his ox or donkey from the stall, and lead it away to water it? So ought not this woman, being a daughter of Abraham, whom Satan has bound—think of it—for eighteen years, be loosed from this bond on the Sabbath?" And when He said these things, all His adversaries were put to shame; and all the multitude rejoiced for all the glorious things that were done by Him. Luke 13:10-17

Jesus broke through the traditions of men and loosed a woman bent over by an infirmity that had bound her eighteen years. Jesus said that Satan bound her. Women have been bound by Satan in many ways since the fall in the Garden of Eden. Jesus sees the condition of women and is calling them to Himself. He is going to loose women so that they can stand tall and take their place in the body of Christ.

Jesus called this woman a daughter of Abraham. This was a radical declaration that she was an heir of salvation through faith. The Pharisees felt they were sons of Abraham, but Jesus told them they were of their father the devil (John

8:44). Religious leaders were constantly offended with what Jesus did. They are going to be greatly offended in the days ahead as Jesus continues loosing women into powerful anointings and leadership giftings. Jesus is going to rip the kingdom out of the hands of sinful men and transfer leadership to the mature sons of God including many women. The power of the Church will increase greatly as women come into their place loosed from years of being heavily yoked by man's oppression.

Jesus laid his hands on women to heal them. To the pure, all things are pure. Religious leaders of Jesus' day were so bound up in impurity that they would never even touch a woman or be seen alone with a woman in public. It is the same today for the religious. They have religious standards to hold them accountable because of their own carnality. It was unthinkable for a Pharisee to touch a woman in prayer. Jesus did it often as He laid hands on the sick to heal them (Mark 1:30,31).

Jesus Allowed Women to Minister to Him

And behold, a woman in the city who was a sinner, when she knew that Jesus sat at the table in the Pharisee's house, brought an alabaster flask of fragrant oil, and stood at His feet behind Him weeping; and she began to wash His feet with her tears, and wiped them with the hair of her head; and she kissed His feet and anointed them with the fragrant oil. Luke 7:37-38

Simon, the Pharisee, did not wash Jesus feet or anoint them with oil. He wanted the honor of dining with Jesus but would not humble himself to provide the hospitality afforded to guests by washing their feet. Perhaps Simon's servants had the day off. We do not know, but a sinful woman gained entrance to the house and washed Jesus' feet with her tears, wiping them with the hair of her head. She kissed His feet and anointed them with fragrant oil.

This woman loved and worshiped Jesus who promptly declared that her sins were forgiven and that her faith had saved her. The Holy Spirit did not release Luke to use the name of this woman. She was a portrait of one who had been forgiven much and consequently loved much. Who will God choose to use in His government in the last days? Will He choose proud Simons who want the honor of supping with Jesus or will He choose redeemed women who have humbled themselves to worship at His feet?

There they made Him a supper; and Martha served, but Lazarus was one of those who sat at the table with Him. Then Mary took a pound of very costly oil of spikenard, anointed the feet of Jesus, and wiped His feet with her hair. And the house was filled with the fragrance of the oil. Then one of His disciples, Judas Iscariot, Simon's son, who would betray Him, said, "Why was this fragrant oil not sold for three hundred denarii and given to the poor?" This he said, not that he cared for the poor, but because he was a thief, and had the money box; and he used to take what was put in it. John 12:2-6

Judas was intensely offended when Mary anointed the feet of Jesus. Jesus allowed Mary to anoint His feet and blessed her for doing so. Judas was indignant and soon would betray Jesus for thirty pieces of silver. Mary lavished her precious oil upon Jesus. This oil was worth a year's wages and was undoubtedly Mary's life savings. She gave everything she had to anoint Jesus. Judas failed to keep his office as apostle because of greed over money. Many Marys of the last-days will qualify for office level positions because of their pure devotion, while greedy Judas types will fall.

The past sins do not matter when it comes to the grace and forgiveness of Jesus. Jesus forgave sinful women and honored them greatly. He is still in the business of restoring wicked sinners. He honors redeemed sinners with great grace to become co-heirs with Himself and have a place of rule and leadership in His house if they will obey. The government is upon His shoulders and He delegates portions of leadership to those who will take His yoke upon their shoulders and walk in perfect agreement with Him. Jesus is no respecter of persons!

Only Men Rejected and Killed Jesus

And this is the condemnation, that the light has come into the world, and men loved darkness rather than light, because their deeds were evil. John 3:19

Undoubtedly, there were women who did not love Jesus or believe in Him, but the New Testament never mentions a woman who rejected or persecuted Jesus during His life. Women wept with agony along the way to the cross. Women were gathered at the cross and did not abandon Jesus in His most difficult moments. Women came to the tomb while the men apostles hid in fear.

All those recorded in the biblical record who opposed Jesus were men. All the religious leaders of Jesus' day were men! The Pharisees, Saducees, scribes and lawyers saw the Light of the world and rejected Him because they loved the darkness of witchcraft control. The Sanhedrin council, who voted to kill Jesus, were all Jewish men. These men led the nation as a whole to reject God incarnate. Only a few religious leaders, like Nicodemus, embraced Jesus. The chief priests and Caiaphas, the High Priest, were all men who rejected and sought to kill Jesus. Judas, a called apostle and a friend to Jesus betrayed Him out of greed. The chief priests were happy to pay Judas money from the temple treasury to betray unto death the One they despised. The male religious leaders were lovers of money and raged against Jesus until they found a way to kill Him. The Roman leaders and soldiers who mocked, whipped, persecuted and killed Jesus were all men. Little has changed over hundreds of years.

Religious men are often ensnared by political aspirations and selfish ambition. Men are often self-focused and insecure. Bound in fear, they long to be in dominant control. Yielding to task orientation, men in ministry often seek to build a big ministry in order to feel good about themselves. Men in ministry today can easily become like the men who opposed Jesus in the first century. Unrighteous men have sought to dominate and control the body of Christ for centuries. They have also consistently excluded all women from positions of leadership in their midst. These misguided men have abused women and have tried to keep them bound up in a religion little better than the Pharisees. With unrighteous bias, men have tampered with the translation of the Scriptures and changed important texts about women. The Lord Himself is going to destroy the works of man's hands and bring His Church into new leadership that is anointed and chosen by the Spirit of God. This will include a host of holy women who are waiting for the Father to promote them!

Jesus Appeared to Women First After His Resurrection

Now after the Sabbath, as the first day of the week began to dawn, Mary Magdalene and the other Mary came to see the tomb. And behold, there was a great earthquake; for an angel of the Lord descended from heaven, and came and rolled back the stone from the door, and sat on it. His countenance was like lightning, and his clothing as white as snow. And the guards shook for fear of him, and became like dead men. But the angel answered and said to the women, "Do not be afraid, for I know that you seek Jesus who was crucified. He is not

here; for He is risen, as He said. Come, see the place where the Lord lay. And go quickly and tell His disciples that He is risen from the dead, and indeed He is going before you into Galilee; there you will see Him. Behold, I have told you." So they went out quickly from the tomb with fear and great joy, and ran to bring His disciples word. And as they went to tell His disciples, behold, Jesus met them, saying, "Rejoice!" So they came and held Him by the feet and worshipped Him. Then Jesus said to them, "Do not be afraid. Go and tell My brethren to go to Galilee, and there they will see Me." Matthew 28:1-10

After raising from the dead, Jesus first appeared to women and gave them a word to give to His disciples. Jesus is the infinite, all wise Creator God. His first post-resurrection action and words were planned according to His wisdom. Jesus chose to appear to women first for a purpose. He demonstrated that He was no respecter of persons. The women were truly devoted to Him. They stood at the cross and watched Jesus in agony while all the disciples fled except John.

Jesus established a New Testament principle by appearing to the women first and giving them a prophetic word. He was including women in a position of honor and leadership in the new kingdom He was establishing. They were to tell the apostles to go to Galilee and there they would see Jesus. This was a directive prophetic word. These kinds of words are generally only given to office level prophets. Jesus' eleven disciples were chosen to be foundational apostles yet they were required to obey the word given to devoted women who had no formal recognition. Do you want to see Jesus in post resurrection form? He is beginning to move powerfully through prophetic women. The disciples were challenged to receive a directive prophetic word from women. They did not believe them and hardened their hearts.

Now when He rose early on the first day of the week,

He appeared first to Mary Magdalene, out of whom He had cast seven demons. She went and told those who had been with Him, as they mourned and wept. And when they heard that He was alive and had been seen by her, they did not believe. After that, He appeared in another form to two of them as they walked and went into the country. And they went and told it to the rest, but they did not believe them either. Later He appeared to the eleven as they sat at the table; and He rebuked their unbelief and hardness of heart, because they did not believe those who had seen Him after He had risen. Mark 16:9-14

The Lord appeared first to Mary Magdalene who is noted to have had seven demons. Mary Magdalene was forgiven much by Jesus and she loved Jesus very much. The honor Jesus bestowed upon Mary is great and is a source of inspiration and hope to all redeemed sinners who have been delivered from much. Mary was graced to have an important word for the apostles and faithfully delivered it in obedience to her Master! The apostles did not believe Mary had seen or heard Jesus. Many godly men today are also rejecting accurate words from women.

Then they returned from the tomb and told all these things to the eleven and to all the rest. It was Mary Magdalene, Joanna, Mary the mother of James, and the other women with them, who told these things to the apostles. And their words seemed to them like idle tales, and they did not believe them. Luke 24:9-11

God is giving many women today prophetic words and revelations of God's truth. Many of these dear women are experiencing the same rejection as Mary Magdalene, Joanna and Mary the mother of James felt. It is important for women to shake off the rejection and keep their hearts in pure mercy towards men who reject them. It is equally important to keep obeying the Lord when He commands women to go and speak to men.

But Mary stood outside by the tomb weeping, and as she wept she stooped down and looked into the tomb. And she saw two angels in white sitting, one at the head and the other at the feet, where the body of Jesus had lain. Then they said to her, "Woman, why are you weeping?" She said to them, "Because they have taken away my Lord, and I do not know where they have laid Him." Now when she had said this, she turned around and saw Jesus standing there, and did not know that it was Jesus. Jesus said to her, "Woman, why are you weeping? Whom are you seeking?" She, supposing Him to be the gardener, said to Him, "Sir, if You have carried Him away, tell me where You have laid Him, and I will take Him away." Jesus said to her, "Mary!" She turned and said to Him, "Rabboni!" (which is to say, Teacher). Jesus said to her, "Do not cling to Me, for I have not yet ascended to My Father; but go to My brethren and say to them, 'I am ascending to My Father and your Father, and to My God and your God.'" Mary Magdalene came and told the disciples that she had seen the Lord, and that He had spoken these things to her. John 20:11-18

Mary loved Jesus and worshipped Him with all her heart. She became a beautiful woman and Jesus loved her deeply. Her sins were forgiven. He graced her by His appearance and allowed her to cling to His feet for a moment. Mary did not immediately recognize Jesus through her tears. There was something so different about His physical appearance. She thought He was the gardener.

The risen Christ can only be known by the Spirit of God. Mary and the two on the road to Emmaus had to recognize Jesus by the Spirit of God. We have to recognize Jesus by the Spirit who confirms a witness to our spirits. When I listen to ministers today, I seek to listen by my spirit as well as my mind. If they are flowing in a pure anointing, I pray to recognize that and receive from them whether they are male or female.

Paul understood that it was important to know people by the Spirit and not by the flesh (II Corinthians 5:16). I used to know people in ministry primarily by mental observations and evaluations of doctrine according to my own orthodoxy. If a person taught things I did not agree with, I would tend to reject everything I heard. If a person had a strange mannerism or came from a different culture, I often had trouble hearing their message. If the person was a woman, she was definitely suspect. God has brought me to much repentance over the past years.

Now I try to know people by the Spirit of God witnessing to my spirit. Once, I was attending a conference and saw a young African man across the room. Immediately, by spirit, I knew He was a zealous believer and I wanted to connect with him. My spirit reached out and saw companionship of like belief even before I met the young man. Later, we became friends and our church now supports his ministry in Togo, West Africa.

When I briefly met Cindy Jacobs, my spirit approved of her spirit and I dreamed a beautiful dream about her that night. I have sat under Cindy's teaching, read her books and profited by submitting to the anointing upon her. Through extensive reading and attending conferences, I have also been blessed by Henrietta Mears, Kay Arthur, Joyce Meyers, Doris Wagner, Patricia King, Heidi Baker, Jill Austin and many other women. I have been inspired by the example of many women through scriptures and a life of serving Jesus on the mission field and in the Church. Women of faith are sons of God!

Women at Pentecost

And when they had entered, they went up into the upper room where they were staying: Peter, James,

**John, and Andrew; Philip and Thomas; Bartholomew
and Matthew; James the son of Alphaeus and Simon the
Zealot; and Judas the son of James. These all continued
with one accord in prayer and supplication, with the
women and Mary the mother of Jesus, and with His
brothers. Acts 1:13-14**

There were one hundred and twenty devoted followers
who tarried in the upper room until the Holy Spirit came at
Pentecost. Women were there including Mary, the mother of
Jesus. Interestingly, Luke adds that Jesus' brothers also
gathered there. Those who had been skeptics at best during
His public ministry were now waiting in fervent prayer for
the promise of the Holy Spirit. Jesus brought His whole
family in on the new birth experience. Apparently Joseph
had died before Jesus' ministry was launched and is not
heard of in scripture again. All focus was to be on the heavenly Father and His victorious Son who was sending the
Holy Spirit.

When the Holy Spirit came, women were anointed, baptized by the Spirit and spoke with other tongues. Mary
Magdalene, Joanna, Susanna and Mary and Martha were
probably there as well. The Spirit poured out and the Church
was birthed. The power of God went forth and the book of
Acts records the first fruits of ministry that exploded in the
first century. The mighty Church of Deborah awoke and
began to sing!

CHAPTER 5

NEW TESTAMENT WOMEN

All Scripture is given by inspiration of God, and is profitable for doctrine, for reproof, for correction, for instruction in righteousness, that <u>the man</u> of God may be complete, thoroughly equipped for every good work. II Timothy 3:16-17 (underlining mine)

God has given the scriptures as a great gift to mankind. This includes, men and women, boys and girls who can read the word of God and learn from the Holy Spirit. Paul wrote that the scriptures were given to equip **"the man of God."** I pray that no Christian today would use this passage to conclude that the Bible was written to equip men only and that women should not be allowed to read the Bible. This was not God's or Paul's intent.

The scriptures can be misunderstood by well meaning people. A man could argue vehemently that the Bible says the purpose of the scriptures is for **"the man of God"** to be complete and equipped, not women. For many hundreds of years, the practice of the Church was to only train men in the word of God to be leaders over the people. Women were not trained in the word of God or allowed to teach in centuries past. This scripture hardly justifies that practice.

Sometimes, men or women, view the scriptures through biased lenses and come to conclusions that God never intended. Most of us have misinterpreted or misunderstood some Bible verses. There are some Bible verses that no one can seem to adequately explain. In some cases, only God knows what was meant. Most of the Scriptures are consistently clear about many things. In some cases, we have "problem passages" that we need to really wrestle with to understand.

Related to women in ministry, there are four primary problem passages that seem to indicate that women should not be allowed to have authority in the Church. We are going to carefully study these passages and see what these passages mean in their context and original language. We need to examine the overall view Paul and John had related to women before we study these four passages. We have already seen that Jesus favored women greatly and was revolutionary in His approach towards women.

All of the controversial passages related to women in ministry are found in Paul's letters to specific situations in Church history. Proper interpretation requires that we know the specific situation before we make a doctrine to apply to all churches in all places throughout all times.

Scripture interpretation bias is a serious matter because it affects the lives of so many people. Historically, there has been enormous gender bias in relationship to women in ministry. A small handful of passages have been taken out of their historical context and applied as absolute doctrine and a resounding "thus says the Lord." There is great treasure in the word of God that has yet to be understood by the unveiling of the Holy Spirit. God intends us to have our eyes opened to the truth that women can be qualified to be His leaders in every aspect of Church government and ministry.

This is seen in the New Testament through Paul's writings as well, once we remove our biased lenses. We'll start by looking at a woman who worked with Paul in ministry.

Phoebe

I commend to you Phoebe our sister, who is a servant of the church in Cenchrea, that you may receive her in the Lord in a manner worthy of the saints, and assist her in whatever business she has need of you; for indeed she has been a helper of many and of myself also. Romans 16:1-2

Paul mentions 29 people in Romans 16 and the first one is a beloved woman named Phoebe. The second person mentioned is Priscilla, a prominent woman. Ten of the persons named in this chapter are women ministers. Paul acknowledged the role of women in the early Church and started a long list of greetings with commendations of two women. We won't build a doctrine on that fact, but it does indicate Paul appreciated women in ministry and the text declares that Phoebe helped Paul in ministry.

Unfortunately, we have to deal with gender bias in the translation. Phoebe was more than **"a servant"** of the church in Cenchrea. The Greek text declares she was a "diakonos," the masculine title meaning "deacon" or "minister." Paul uses the word "diakonos" 21 times and it is translated minister 18 times, deacon two times and servant one time. It was translated "servant" to describe Phoebe due to the gender bias of the translators. Phoebe was an anointed minister of the church in Cenchrea. She was a prominent leader whom Paul recognized and gave her the proper title "diakonos."

There are a number of non-biblical sources that state that there were women ministers in the early Church into the fourth century AD. Diakonos, both men and women, served as prophets and teachers in the early Church.

Paul commended Phoebe as one who had been a **"helper of many"** including himself. The word "prostatis" (used only once) is translated "helper" but also may mean "patroness or guardian" and comes from the root word "proistemi" meaning "to manage or conduct" and is translated "to maintain, be over or rule." Proistemi is used of leadership functions in Romans 12:8, I Thessalonians 5:12 and I Timothy 3:4,5,12. As Paul commends Phoebe for her help, the word use in the Greek implies that her help was at a significant leadership level as one would expect from a prominent diakonos.

If there was no translation bias in Romans 16:1,2, it could revolutionize the way we view women. Romans 16:1,2 could be translated, **"I commend to you Phoebe our sister, who is a minister of the church in Cenchrea, that you may receive her in the Lord in a manner worthy of the saints, and assist her in whatever business she has need of you; for indeed she has been a ministering influence over many and of myself also"**

Paul told the Romans to assist Phoebe in whatever she needed them to do for her business. Phoebe's business was to conduct ministry and she was a servant leader to many people and even provided some servant leadership to Paul. He was not ashamed to acknowledge that Phoebe had significantly "helped" him. That's probably why Paul mentioned her first in his list of greetings.

Priscilla and Aquila

Greet Priscilla and Aquila, my fellow workers in Christ Jesus, who risked their own necks for my life, to whom not only I give thanks, but also all the churches of the Gentiles. Likewise greet the church that is in their house. Romans 16:3-5a

Priscilla was a New Testament woman leader who was married to Aquila. They had a church in their home, which they pastored. Priscilla's name is mentioned first indicating that she was probably the more dynamic leader of the two when it came to things of the Spirit. Priscilla was a teacher who instructed the great orator Apollos. This was no small matter. Apollos was a powerful leader who knew the Scriptures extremely well.

Meanwhile a Jew named Apollos, a native of Alexandria, came to Ephesus. He was a learned man, with a thorough knowledge of the Scriptures. He had been instructed in the way of the Lord, and he spoke with great fervor and taught about Jesus accurately, though he knew only the baptism of John. He began to speak boldly in the synagogue. When Priscilla and Aquila heard him, they invited him to their home and explained to him the way of God more adequately.

When Apollos wanted to go to Achaia, the brothers encouraged him and wrote to the disciples there to welcome him. On arriving, he was a great help to those who by grace had believed. For he vigorously refuted the Jews in public debate, proving from the Scriptures that Jesus was the Christ. Acts 18:24-28 NIV

Luke joined Paul in listing Priscilla's name first when instructing Apollos more accurately since Apollos only knew of the baptism of John. I quoted the Acts verse above in the NIV because the NKJV exhibits a gender bias in the translation of the Greek. Priscilla's name is listed first in the original manuscripts but due to gender bias, some English versions put Aquila's name first. This was not changed in Romans 16:3. The translator bias came as a result of believing that a woman could not teach a man so that Aquila was listed first to indicate that he taught Apollos. In Romans 16, the greeting doesn't carry the same kind of weight so the bias wasn't employed.

It appears that Priscilla had leadership prominence in the early Church and risked her neck to help Paul. Her fame was well known to many Gentile churches. Priscilla was at least a five-fold teacher in the body of Christ and may have been an apostle, pastor and evangelist also.

Junia

Greet Andronicus and Junia, my countrymen and my fellow prisoners, who are of note among the apostles, who also were in Christ before me. Romans 16:7

Junia was probably the wife of Andronicus and Paul greets her with four designations. Junia was a countryman, a fellow prisoner, a fellow apostle and was in Christ before Paul. Junia was a common female name in the Roman Empire and the Church Fathers recognized her as a woman. Gender bias led later translators to call her Junias, explaining that it was an abbreviation of the Latin name "Junianus," a man.

The Church Father, John Chrysostom (died 407 AD), who had a negative view of women in many cases, understood "Junia" in Romans 16:7 as a woman and was amazed that she could be called an apostle: "Oh how great is the devotion of this woman, that she should be even counted worthy of the appellation of apostle!" (St. John Chrysostom, Homily 31 on Romans 16:5-16, The Nicene and Post-Nicene Fathers, Series 1, vol. 9, Grand Rapids: Eerdmans, 1971-1980). The first commentator to understand "Junia" as the hypothetical masculine name "Junias" was Aegidius of Rome in the 14th century AD (D. Scholer, Theology News and Notes, March 1995,p. 22). A great deal of effort has been made by biased scholars to deny that Junia was a woman or an apostle because if she was recognized by Paul as an apostle, all five-fold offices would be open to women.

Women Elders

Rebuke not an elder, but intreat him as a father; and the younger men as brethren; The elder women as mothers; the younger as sisters, with all purity. I Timothy 5:1,2 KJV

Paul exhorts us not to rebuke an elder and uses the Greek word "presbuterio" the masculine form for elder. In talking of the women, Paul calls them "presbuterai," the female form for elder. Translators often assume the passage is only talking about older men or older women but in the same chapter, Paul uses the masculine form "presbuterio" to indicate the church office of elder.

Let the <u>elders</u> who rule well be counted worthy of double honor, especially those who labor in the word and doctrine. For the Scripture says, "You shall not muzzle an ox while it treads out the grain," and, "The laborer is worthy of his wages." Do not receive an accusation against an <u>elder</u> except from two or three witnesses. I Timothy 5:17-19 (underlining mine)

The fact that the masculine form for elder in the verse above refers to the office of elder who ruled the household of God and taught the word of God suggests that the same word in I Timothy 5:1,2 in both the masculine and feminine forms refers to ruling elders as well. This is consistent in the context of Paul's writing. The women elders are to be treated as mothers and given the honor associated with those who teach and impart the wisdom of God as we noted in Chapter 2. If I Timothy 5:1,2 was consistently translated it would state, **"Rebuke not a male ruling elder, but intreat him as a father; and the younger men as brethren; The women ruling elders as mothers; the younger as sisters, with all purity."**

There is substantial archeological evidence that there

were women elders alongside the male elders. In early church history, Irvin notes that in Egypt, a 2nd-3rd century inscription refers to a woman named "Paniskanes" as a presbutera or "female elder" (D. Irvin, "The Ministry of Women in the Early Church: The Archaeological Evidence," Duke Divinity School Review 2 [1980]: 76-86). Bishop Diognenes set up a memorial to a woman in the 3rd century named "Amonnian the female elder (presbutera)." In Rome, the 4th century Basilica of Prudentiana and Praxedis contains a mosaic including a woman referred to as "Bishop Theodora" (Episcopa Theodora). At about 363 AD, the Council of Laodicea stopped the practice of ordaining women elders and decreed that it was wrong for women to be elders and teach men (Nicene and Post-Nicene Fathers, Series II, Vol. XIV [Grand Rapids: Eerdmans, 1971-1980]). By the fact of this council's decision, this is confirmation that there were women elders in the early Church for over 300 years who also taught men.

"For by it the elders obtained a good testimony" (Hebrews 11:2). In the book of Hebrews, the Greek term "elders" (presbuteroi) was used to refer to those who had obtained a good testimony through faith and obedience. Among these elders, we find several women including Sarah (Hebrews 11:11,13), Moses' mother (Hebrews 11:23), Rahab (Hebrews 11:31) and the woman of Zaraphath (I Kings 17:17-24; Hebrews 11:35). These elders are part of the great cloud of witnesses and include women (Hebrews 12:1).

The Elect Lady

THE ELDER, To the elect lady and her children, whom I love in truth, and not only I, but also all those who have known the truth, because of the truth which abides in us and will be with us forever: Grace, mercy, and peace will be with you from God the Father and

from the Lord Jesus Christ, the Son of the Father, in truth and love.

I rejoiced greatly that I have found <u>some of your children</u> walking in truth, as we received commandment from the Father. And now I plead with you, lady, not as though I wrote a new commandment to you, but that which we have had from the beginning: that we love one another. This is love, that we walk according to His commandments. This is the commandment, that as you have heard from the beginning, you should walk in it.

For many deceivers have gone out into the world who do not confess Jesus Christ as coming in the flesh. This is a deceiver and an antichrist. Look to yourselves, that we do not lose those things we worked for, but that we may receive a full reward. Whoever transgresses and does not abide in the doctrine of Christ does not have God. He who abides in the doctrine of Christ has both the Father and the Son. If anyone comes to you and does not bring this doctrine, do not receive him into your house nor greet him; for he who greets him shares in his evil deeds.

Having many things to write to you, I did not wish to do so with paper and ink; but I hope to come to you and speak face to face, that our joy may be full. The children of your elect sister greet you. Amen. II John (underlining mine)

The apostle John wrote this precious letter to a woman minister whom he calls the elect lady. She was the gatekeeper over her household church. The New Testament writings are instructional for the whole Church. The Church Fathers did not decide on a whim to include John's note to some lady whose children he had met. This authentic letter was written to a woman who was exhorted to keep false teachers and prophets out of her home.

This elect lady was responsible to discern true and false

teaching that could affect her "children." John uses the word "children" fourteen times in his first letter (see I John) and it always refers to the believers who had put their trust in Jesus Christ. **"My little children, let us not love in word or in tongue, but in deed and in truth" (I John 3:18).** John was an elder and "father" who took the responsibility of watching over his "children" in the faith very seriously. "Children" is a clear reference to those believers John had leadership over. In John's third letter, he uses children one time as he states, **"I have no greater joy than to hear that my children walk in truth" (III John 4).** In all three of John's letters, the word children is used to describe disciples of Jesus Christ who had come under John's care or the care of the elect lady. John also mentions, **"The children of your elect sister greet you" (II John 13).** If we use the interpretation of **"children"** consistently in this passage, this elect lady had an anointed sister who also had a house church that John knew of and ministered to. The disciples of the elect sister sent greetings with John's letter. This inclusion is a great affirmation of the valuable ministry of women by the apostle John.

It is consistent with John's epistles that the "children" he is referring to with the elect lady are those she had led to the Lord and oversaw in the church she conducted in her home. Paul also used the term "children" to refer to church members or disciples (see I Corinthians 4:14; II Corinthians 12:14; Galatians 4:19; I Thessalonians 2:7). The elect lady that John addresses apparently ran this church by herself. She may have been single or more likely widowed.

Other women in the New Testament had house churches including Lydia (Acts 16:14,15,40), Chloe (I Corinthians 1:11), Nympha (Colossians 4:15), Apphia (and her husband Philemon, Philemon 2) and Priscilla (and Aquila, Romans 16:3-5).

Paul certainly knew the Old Testament references to

women in leadership and knew women leaders like Phoebe and Priscilla whom he commended. Paul recognized that women were praying and prophesying in church as well as teaching (I Corinthians 11:5; Acts 18:26). Therefore, the few difficult passages that Paul writes must be interpreted in light of the evidence advocating women in leadership and teaching roles. Let's take a closer look at these challenging passages.

A Man, the Husband of One Wife

This is a faithful saying: If a man desires the position of a bishop, he desires a good work. A bishop then must be blameless, the husband of one wife, temperate, sober-minded, of good behavior, hospitable, able to teach; I Timothy 3:1,2

For this reason I left you in Crete, that you should set in order the things that are lacking, and appoint elders in every city as I commanded you—if a man is blameless, the husband of one wife, having faithful children not accused of dissipation or insubordination. For a bishop must be blameless, as a steward of God, not self-willed, not quick-tempered, not given to wine, not violent, not greedy for money. Titus 1:5-7

One earnest man who loves God told me bluntly that an elder must be the husband of one wife and therefore no woman could ever be an elder. Case closed. End of discussion! He was so dogmatic and determined with his view that I decided not to respond. Under his standards, Jesus Himself would not have qualified to be an elder in the Church because He was not married.

"If a man ("tis" in Greek) desires the position of a bishop." The New King James Bible decided along with the

King James Bible to translate the Greek word "tis" as "a man." However, the Greek word "tis" is both feminine and masculine in its gender reference and this is common knowledge in all introductory Greek grammars. The NIV accurately translates "tis" as "anyone." The translators of the King James Bible occasionally exhibited a gender bias that existed in that time.

John 3:3 uses the word "tis" when describing who can be born again. **"Jesus answered and said to him, 'Most assuredly, I say to you, unless one (tis) is born again, he cannot see the kingdom of God.'"** The KJV is consistent by translating this as "man" whereas the NKJV and NIV accurately translated "tis" as "one." No reasonable scholar would conclude from John 3:3 that only men can be born again by placing their faith in Jesus Christ. The Greek word "tis" means "anyone, anybody, whoever." I Timothy 3:1 is more accurately rendered **"If anyone desires to be an overseer..."** This opens the possibility for women to be overseers once again.

Some would argue that the word for overseer is a masculine plural form and this is true. But it is consistent throughout scriptures that titles are not used with both masculine and female or neuter forms. Titles are primarily masculine forms. Deborah was considered a judge in Israel. The word for "judge" used to describe her was a masculine plural form of the Hebrew word "shofetim" (Judges 2:16). Phoebe and other women were included with men under the masculine Greek title "diakonos" in Romans 16:1 and I Timothy 3:8,11. Junia was included with Andronicus and other men under the plural Greek title "apostles" (Greek masculine plural dative "apostolois") in Romans 16:7. The masculine form of a title does not exclude women from that office.

The **"husband of but one wife"** seals it for many believers with a certainty that women can't be leaders in the Church. As said above, that would exclude all single men and Jesus Himself from being a leader in the Church. That passage alone disqualifies all Catholic priests! What was Paul's intent here? What was the specific situation that Timothy was dealing with in Ephesus? Were there men who had two or more wives that became believers? If anyone could be a bishop, either male or female, then the prohibition was to keep men who had multiple wives from being in leadership. Women have rarely been known historically to have more than one husband but men have often had multiple wives. The passage is simply not conclusive to build a doctrine of excluding women from leadership.

Let your Women Keep Silent in the Churches

For God is not the author of confusion but of peace, as in all the churches of the saints. Let your women keep silent in the churches, for they are not permitted to speak; but they are to be submissive, as the law also says. And if they want to learn something, let them ask their own husbands at home; for it is shameful for women to speak in church. I Corinthians 14:33-35

This passage appears to forbid women from speaking in public worship. But look what Paul taught earlier in the same book. **"But every woman who prays or prophesies with her head uncovered dishonors her head, for that is one and the same as if her head were shaved" (I Corinthians 11:5).** Paul acknowledged in this verse that women prayed and prophesied in the public service so why would he later say that women could not speak in church? He taught that women should have their head covered when they prayed or prophesied, apparently an important ancient cultural exhortation but not applicable to all women for all times. Paul allowed women to pray and prophesy in his meetings. So what does it mean in I Corinthians 14:35 that women are to be silent?

First of all, the Greek word translated "women" is "gunaikes" which should be translated "wives" as the mention of "husbands" in the same verse requires. The context of this passage found in I Corinthians 14:26-39 suggests that husbands were involved in judging prophecies and that their wives were interrupting by speaking to them out of order. The wives were bringing a liberty they had at home in private with their husbands into a church assembly context. Paul exhorts the people three times in this passage to "keep silent." The most famous of the three is quoted above. Let's look at the other two.

But if there is no interpreter, <u>let him keep silent</u> in church, and let him speak to himself and to God. Let two or three prophets speak, and let the others judge. But if anything is revealed to another who sits by, <u>let the first keep silent</u>. 1 Corinthians 14:28-30 (underlining mine)

Paul was dealing with order in the church related to the exercise of the gifts of the Holy Spirit, which are to be exercised for the edification of the body. The Corinthians were extremely gifted but were also immature and needed structure. Paul taught that no one should interrupt the service with the release of a tongue unless there was an interpreter present who could give the interpretation. In the case of prophets speaking, others were to judge. If one who is judging the prophecy is waiting on the Lord and receiving something, the one who gave the word is exhorted to remain silent.

In the context of this passage on discerning prophetic words, apparently some wives were asking their husbands questions or making comments that was disrupting the flow of the anointing. Paul taught them to respect the order of the service and wait until they got home to ask questions rather than disturb the prophetic flow. Paul was not talking to all women of all times, he was speaking of certain wives who were out of order in the Corinthian Church of the first century.

I do not Permit a Woman
to Teach or to Have Authority over a Man

I desire therefore that the men pray everywhere, lifting up holy hands, without wrath and doubting; in like manner also, that the women adorn themselves in modest apparel, with propriety and moderation, not with braided hair or gold or pearls or costly clothing, but, which is proper for women professing godliness, with good works. Let a woman learn in silence with all submission. And I do not permit a woman to teach or to have authority over a man, but to be in silence. For Adam was formed first, then Eve. And Adam was not deceived, but the woman being deceived, fell into transgression. Nevertheless she will be saved in childbearing if they continue in faith, love, and holiness, with self-control. I Timothy 2:8-15

At first glance at this passage, one could easily conclude that Paul wanted the men to lift up their hands and pray and do all the ministry and women to dress modestly and keep quiet. That sums up many churches' interpretation of this passage for the past centuries. Paul already recognized that women prayed and prophesied in church meetings (I Corinthians 11:5). Paul's intent was not just for the men to pray and the women to sit quietly and look proper. Paul said, **"in like manner also"** meaning the women were to also lift up their holy hands and pray. For the men, Paul says they are to pray **"without wrath and doubting."** The women are exhorted to pray adorned with **"modest apparel."** Again these were specific applications to a situation that was occurring that Timothy had communicated to Paul.

At face value, this passage seems to clinch the argument for any believer with a common understanding of the English language. That again is the problem. We are studying the

Bible in English, which was translated from Greek. Once you understand the Greek rendering of this verse, it will help you understand what Paul was saying.

A better rendering of the Greek text according to Dr. Gary Grieg is **"I am not permitting a woman/wife to teach or to domineer a man/husband."** The Greek verb "authentein" means "to domineer" not simply to "exercise authority." Paul is not disallowing all women in Ephesus from teaching and exercising any kind of authority over men in general, because Paul certainly knew Priscilla, who had been one of his co-workers in Ephesus and that she and her husband taught Apollos in Acts 18:26.

Paul was not talking about "women" in plural as he was earlier in I Timothy 2:9,10. In I Timothy 2:11-15 he speaks of "a woman" in the singular, referring to one woman or at most a small number of women at Ephesus.

Then suddenly, Paul shifts emphasis to declare that Adam was formed first and that Eve was deceived and that women will be saved in childbearing. Many have interpreted this to mean that "a woman's place is in the home." Certainly God wants wives to bear children and raise children in godly fear. But what was Paul after here?

In ancient Ephesus there was a "goddess of Eve" cult that taught that Eve was formed first and that she was the mother of us all. This cult led women to take dominion over their husbands and be domineering and bossy. They taught that Eve was the source of knowledge and wisdom, which she got from the serpent. Apparently, one of the women in the church Timothy led was influenced by this cult and was causing a stir. Paul counteracts the lies of this cult by declaring that Adam was formed first not Eve. And it was Eve who fell into deception.

God declares that the husband is the head of the household and wives are not to dominate and take the place of leadership over their husbands in household headship. Paul was dealing with a specific problem that Timothy undoubtedly mentioned to him. In response, perhaps Paul was saying, "I would not let that woman dominate her husband or interrupt the service with her false views." Let's look at this passage again.

Let a woman learn in silence with all submission. And I do not permit a woman to teach or to have authority over a man, but to be in silence. For Adam was formed first, then Eve. And Adam was not deceived, but the woman being deceived, fell into transgression. Nevertheless she will be saved in childbearing if they continue in faith, love, and holiness, with self-control. I Timothy 2:11-15

The Greek word "hesuchia" is translated "silence" in this passage. Hesuchia means a quietness, a lack of hustle and bustle and refers to a state of peace. Paul was not saying that women could not speak or ask any questions whatsoever. There was a raging controversy in Ephesus due to false doctrine in this Eve cult. Paul wanted the women to learn and trust Timothy's leadership. It would take some time for Timothy to carefully instruct them in all the word of God that was needed to establish their faith and counteract the Eve cult. Paul was encouraging the women to be patient and learn in quietness with an inner attitude of trust.

Furthermore, Paul simply corrected the incorrect teaching of the Eve cult by stating that Adam was formed first and then Eve. It was believed in that Gnostic cult that Eve was the originator of man and had the "true knowledge." In this context the Greek word "authentein" could be better translated, **"I am not allowing a woman to teach or to proclaim herself the originator of man. Adam was formed first and then Eve..."** We don't know everything about this passage or Paul's exact meaning, but he was addressing a specific, troubling situation with an emerging cult of Gnosticism. There was a woman or wife who was either extremely domineering and talkative or full of cultic ideas that wanted to be heard. Paul was instructing her to learn in quietness and submission so as to receive correction and sound doctrine. Once you understand this basic context, the passage does not apply to all women for all time. It certainly does apply to some bossy, intrusive women with false doctrines at certain times.

The four passages of Paul we have discussed above have been used as a basis for doctrinal gender bias for hundreds of years. Those passages were written to speak to specific issues to specific churches that existed in the first century A.D. With all the evidence we have studied until now, it should be clear that God has always intended for women to be "mothers" of the faith and have positions of leadership and influence in His kingdom. This includes office levels of leadership in the church.

This truth has been veiled in part by the Holy Spirit but has also been hidden by the gender bias of men who began to take control of the Church in the late fourth century. The Church still needs reformation to come to the place God has for her in the last days. The inclusion of women in leadership is a vital part of that reformation!

CHAPTER 6

INTRODUCING DEBORAH

For this reason I bow my knees to the Father of our Lord Jesus Christ, from whom the whole family in heaven and earth is named. Ephesians 3:14-15

Paul declared that the Father appoints names to every family in heaven and earth. God is absolutely sovereign over the affairs of the spiritual and natural realm. All of the names of people and places in the Bible have significance. A biblical name usually reflects the essential characteristics or nature of the person or place named. In order to begin to understand the prophetic significance of the story of Deborah for today, we need to recognize the hidden treasure of prophetic names that are given in the story.

And I have declared to them Your <u>name</u>, and will declare it, that the love with which You loved Me may be in them, and I in them. John 17:26 (underlining mine)

Jesus declared the name of the Father to His disciples. Jesus taught His disciples the nature of the Father by modeling and teaching that very nature. A thorough study of the names of God throughout scripture enables us to develop the knowledge of God and pursue an intimate relationship with Him through faith.

The name of Jesus has been exalted above all names. Jesus means "Jehovah is salvation, Jehovah, my salvation; Savior." Cornwall and Smith list nearly 300 additional names and titles for Jesus including, "Alpha and Omega, Bridegroom, Chief Cornerstone, Christ Jesus, Good Shepherd, Immanuel, King of Glory, Lord of Hosts, Prince of Peace, Son of God, Son of Man, The True Vine and Wonderful."

Knowing God is a lifelong pursuit of knowing His name. As we behold Him in His nature and experience the revelation of His Person, we are transformed from glory to glory (II Corinthians 3:18). There is a price to pay in terms of prayer, fasting and Bible study to enter into the revelation of the name of God. It is well worth the time and effort. We can only know God by the Holy Spirit as He reveals the name of God to our spirit man and that understanding flows to our minds as revelation. The most important focus anyone can have is to gaze intently upon the Lord and know His name.

In addition, the Lord does not want us to perish because of a lack of knowledge of the ways of the enemy. It is not healthy to focus long periods of time on the enemy or his names, but it is important to know his schemes in order to overcome him. In the story of Deborah, Jabin and Sisera are the names of the enemies of God's people. God recorded their names and the places they came from to give us prophetic clues into their nature and how they would work to enslave God's people. As we carefully study their names, a resource of knowledge is unlocked so that we can see the demonic spirits that worked behind them and recognize how they work in our world today.

As I study the names in the original languages, there are often root words that make up those names. I study the root words and sometimes use an Englishman's concordance that shows all the verses where that exact word is used in the Bible. Word studies are fascinating to me and I enjoy searching for the hidden treasures of the word of God. David sang the truth that God has placed in my heart, **"I rejoice at Your word as one who finds great treasure" (Psalm 119:162).** The word of God is an immense field filled with hidden treasures. As one digs through prayer and study, the Holy Spirit enables us to unearth gems. There are incredible layers of treasures in the word of God.

"For You have magnified Your word above all Your name" (Psalm 138:2b). God has magnified His word above all of His name. God has based His relationship with mankind on the release of His voice, His inspired word. "Rhema" is a Greek word that is translated "word" in the New Testament. "Logos" is a Greek word also translated "word" in the New Testament. Logos is used many more times than rhema. Receiving an inspired "rhema" word from God is a powerful experience that changes your life forever.

God's "logos" is the entire written word that you can read every day. "Rhema" word happens when God breathes on a scripture and brings it to life in your heart speaking deeper revelation. Rhema word is the release of revelation that can enable faith. Paul noted that **"faith comes by hearing, and hearing by the word of God" (Romans 10:17).** "Rhema" is translated "word" in this verse, and it means God's voice on His scriptures. Some people read the Bible every day who do not have true faith in Jesus Christ. They may not even hear His voice as they read the logos. It is absolutely vital that we each pursue the Lord to hear and obey His voice in the scriptures.

In the story of Deborah with all the names and interpretation of names, it is important to pray and ask the Holy Spirit to speak to you by revelation of the Spirit. My prayer has been to listen to the Holy Spirit as I have done the research and to allow the Spirit to teach me the prophetic meanings of the names. The names and places are listed by the inspiration of the Holy Spirit. There is an anointing and purpose for those names to be listed in the Bible. The research and interpretations that I apply to the names are not inspired as the scriptures are, but I pray that they are accurate in bringing forth true revelation that is in agreement with the whole counsel of God and will edify the body of Christ. In order to glean the treasures of the chapters ahead, we are going to have to do some serious digging. Grab your shovel and let's go!

Background to Deborah

Now it shall come to pass, if you diligently obey the voice of the LORD your God, to observe carefully all His commandments which I command you today, that the LORD your God will set you high above all nations of the earth. And all these blessings shall come upon you and overtake you, because you obey the voice of the LORD your God. Deuteronomy 28:1,2

But it shall come to pass, if you do not obey the voice of the LORD your God, to observe carefully all His commandments and His statutes which I command you today, that all these curses will come upon you and overtake you. Deuteronomy 28:15

God's covenant promise to His people was simple. Hear and obey My voice and you will be blessed! Ignore or disobey My voice and you will be cursed! Although we are not under the Law given to Moses, we are to be subject to the law of the Spirit of life in Christ Jesus (Romans 8:1-14). The principle of hearing and obeying God's voice unto blessing is consistent throughout the word of God. Abraham, the father of faith, heard and obeyed God's voice and was blessed.

The Lord God called Abraham out of Ur and as he obeyed, God led him to the land of Canaan. God promised to give this land to Abraham's descendants. After 430 years in Egypt including years of slavery, God's people cried out for deliverance. God sent Moses and delivered the people out of Egypt with His awesome power.

In the wilderness wandering that followed, the Lord gave Moses and His people the covenant of His Law that was to guide the nation until Christ came to fulfill the Law. Under the Law, the Lord established blessings for obeying His voice and curses if they disobeyed His voice. The people of God followed Joshua into the land and conquered portions of the land, but they did not fully drive the enemy out or completely occupy what God promised them.

After Joshua died, the nation entered a time where **"everyone did what was right in his own eyes" (Judges 17:6; 21:25).** The people of God failed to remember the Law given to Moses and turned their hearts to other gods. They refused to seek God and listen to His voice as recorded in Deuteronomy. Therefore, God's curse came into operation and enemies came against God's people and brought them into subjection. God's word is absolute truth. The Israelites disobeyed His voice and the curses were released exactly as God said.

Once the people began to groan under the heavy oppression of the enemy, they started to cry out to God for deliverance. They began the process of repenting and believing in God to send a deliverer. God then raised up a judge with the anointing to deliver the nation out of idolatry and turn their hearts wholly back to Him. The anointed judge often led violent warfare to drive out the invading force and restored the land to peace under God's blessing. After that judge died, the people went back into idolatry and started the cycle over again. There are twelve different judges named in the book of Judges and there were at least twelve cycles of idolatry, oppression, repentance and deliverance that occurred during that 450 year time period (Acts 13:20). This pattern has continued in some measure throughout Church history.

The Office of a Judge

You shall appoint judges and officers in all your gates, which the LORD your God gives you, according to your tribes, and they shall judge the people with just judgment. Deuteronomy 16:18

God told Moses to appoint judges and officers in all the gates of the cities which the Lord was going to give them. Judges were responsible to know the word of God and be righteous and just as they settled the disputes of the people. Local judges were wise elders who ruled over the affairs of the town. Moses was a national judge as was Samuel.

And Samuel judged Israel all the days of his life. He went from year to year on a circuit to Bethel, Gilgal, and Mizpah, and judged Israel in all those places. But he always returned to Ramah, for his home was there. There he judged Israel, and there he built an altar to the LORD. I Samuel 7:15-17

Samuel was a holy priest, prophet and judge. He was a great man of God who ruled the nation in righteousness until the appointment of the kings. Samuel's sons were appointed as local judges but were corrupt. There were national and local judges. The judges in the Book of Judges were anointed men and women of God who were raised up by God for a national role. This is an important factor as we recognize that Deborah was a judge at the highest possible level. She was a judge over the entire nation of Israel.

Nevertheless, the LORD raised up judges who delivered them out of the hand of those who plundered them. Yet they would not listen to their judges, but they played

the harlot with other gods, and bowed down to them. They turned quickly from the way in which their fathers walked, in obeying the commandments of the LORD; they did not do so. And when the LORD raised up judges for them, the LORD was with the judge and delivered them out of the hand of their enemies all the days of the judge; for the LORD was moved to pity by their groaning because of those who oppressed them and harassed them. And it came to pass, when the judge was dead, that they reverted and behaved more corruptly than their fathers, by following other gods, to serve them and bow down to them. They did not cease from their own doings nor from their stubborn way. Judges 2:16-19

God raised up national warrior judges to deliver the people out of the hand of their enemies. The judge had a powerful anointing of God to bring the people back into the fear of the Lord. God chose Deborah to be the fourth judge listed in the book of Judges. She was a national warrior judge who had great authority over the nation. Judges needed to understand the Law and walk in obedience to it at all times.

The Law of Moses was applied to the nation of Israel as the covenant people of God. It was God's covenant law that instituted real blessings or curses depending on the behavior of the people. The intent of God was to form a nation of priests to constrain His people from sin and tutor them until Christ would come and bring redemption from sin and enable God to place His Spirit in their inmost being. God always intended His people to become a holy royal priesthood.

Many teachers and preachers today will boldly say, "We are no longer under the Law." That statement is often misunderstood and misstated. God's laws are still operational in the spiritual realm even though Jesus Himself fulfilled the Law of Moses. Jesus fulfilled every requirement of the Old Covenant Law during His earthly life. He is the only Person who ever did. The principles in the Law did not stop operating just because Jesus perfectly fulfilled the requirements of God's Law.

A New Covenant was created by the sacrifice of Jesus in which we can have our sin nature transformed by the indwelling presence of the Holy Spirit as we place our faith in Jesus and obey His voice. This process includes death to self and life to God. It involves taking up our cross and following Jesus. The flesh nature must be placed in subjection to the Spirit of God in order to be crucified with Christ so that Christ's very nature can emerge from our inmost being.

The Law of the Spirit

There is therefore now no condemnation to those who are in Christ Jesus, who do not walk according to the flesh, but according to the Spirit. For the law of the Spirit of life in Christ Jesus has made me free from the law of sin and death. Romans 8:1-2

Christians who say we are no longer under the "Law" often misunderstand this famous passage. We are no longer called to live by the Law of Moses, but we are now called to live by the **"law of the Spirit of life in Christ Jesus."** The Law of Moses dealt with external issues like "do not commit adultery, do not steal, do not commit murder" and so forth. Jesus taught us that the law of the Spirit did not allow for lust, covetousness or negative speech towards a brother (see Matthew 5-7). The old law dealt with externals, but the new law of the Spirit deals with heart issues.

The law of the Spirit is to be yoked in perfect agreement with Jesus by the presence of the Holy Spirit in our hearts. God wants our hearts to be in agreement with His heart. When our heart is in agreement with His heart, we walk in the Spirit at all times. We are the people of God and are called to obey the voice of the Holy Spirit at all times. God is in us both to will and to work for His good pleasure. It is His good pleasure that we walk as Jesus walked. The Holy Spirit will lead us to conform to the image of Jesus and we will grow to be more like Him over time. Sons of God live by the Spirit of God. We are called to walk in the Spirit at all times and not in the flesh.

When a Christian uses the excuse, "I'm not under the Law" to condone carnal behavior, she is disobeying the law of the Spirit of life in Christ Jesus and is walking according to the flesh. **"For if you live according to the flesh you will die; but if by the Spirit you put to death the deeds of the body, you will live" (Romans 8:13).**

The relentless cycle of carnality and deliverance seen in the book of Judges can be observed in Church history as well. God raises up reformers in Church history to deliver the Church out of false doctrines and carnal practices. The Church in America is filled with carnality and many have turned the grace of our Lord Jesus Christ into a toleration of lewdness. Jude had some extremely harsh words to say about people like that.

These are spots in your love feasts, while they feast with you without fear, serving only themselves. They are clouds without water, carried about by the winds; late autumn trees without fruit, twice dead, pulled up by the roots; raging waves of the sea, foaming up their own shame; wandering stars for whom is reserved the blackness of darkness forever. Jude 12,13

Jesus said that **"many"** who performed amazing ministry activities like prophecy, deliverance and signs would be lost on the Day of Judgment because they did not obey His will (Matthew 7:21). Jude saw this condemnation coming on many sensual individuals who infiltrated the Church with their toleration of immorality. They turned the grace of God into a toleration of fleshly behavior and have twisted the word of God to their own destruction.

Paul taught us that the pattern seen in the Old Testament was a possibility for today. Most Christians have been so deceived by false teaching related to salvation that they cannot even perceive the truth of Paul's words below.

And if some of the branches were broken off, and you, being a wild olive tree, were grafted in among them, and with them became a partaker of the root and fatness of the olive tree, do not boast against the branches. But if you do boast, remember that you do not support the root, but the root supports you. You will say then, "Branches were broken off that I might be grafted in." Well said. Because of unbelief they were broken off, and you stand by faith. Do not be haughty, but fear. For if God did not spare the natural branches, He may not spare you either. Therefore consider the goodness and severity of God: on those who fell, severity; but toward you, goodness, if you continue in His goodness. Otherwise you also will be cut off. Romans 11:17-22

Most of the natural branches of Israel were broken off in the first century because most Israelites rejected faith in Jesus Christ. A remnant of Jews believed in Jesus and continued in the faith of Abraham and his seed of promise. Paul admonished the believers in Rome not to be proud but to fear God. If God did not spare most of the natural branches, He may not spare most of the Church people today. If you live according to the flesh, you will die.

Many "Christians" live by the soul realm of natural reason rather than by revelation from the Spirit of God to the human spirit. When you live by the soul realm as a "Christian," you are living a cultural form of Christianity that is carnal, fleshly and demonic. As a result, carnal "Christians" who live by the soul realm are living by religion, which is a form of the Law of Moses, rather than an intimate relationship with Jesus Christ, hearing and obeying the Holy Spirit. Even though they may say, "we are not living under the Law," because they live in religion, that religion becomes a law and they may be branches about to be broken off. A branch that lives by religion cannot bear fruit and Jesus said that branches that did not bear fruit would be cut off and thrown into the fire (John 15:6).

The book of Judges is extremely relevant for the Church today. We have many people who are declaring that they are Christians, but they are living in lawlessness and are ungoverned by the Holy Spirit. I have written an entire book on this topic called **THE NARROW GATE,** which every Christian leader should read.

Jesus went up on a mountaintop to preach to a select group of individuals from Israel who made the effort to hike up the mountain to hear Him teach. We know this as the Sermon on the Mount. In this message, Jesus' teaching transitions from the Old Covenant to the New Covenant. Jesus knew the hearts of the religious Jews who came to hear Him. He said that the gate was narrow that led to life and that only a few would find it (see Matthew 7:13-23). Jesus said the way was difficult and that many would be turned away on Judgment Day because they practiced lawlessness.

Jesus was talking to the most religious public of all times. Jesus is talking to the "Church" today in the same tone. Many are attending churches that are living on the broad way leading to destruction. Many are performing religious activities thinking that will save them, but the Spirit of God does not lead them nor are they putting to death the deeds of the flesh. The Church needs judges today to rise up in the spirit of Deborah to set them free from Jabins and Siseras who speak from many pulpits.

The Setting for Deborah

When Ehud was dead, the children of Israel again did evil in the sight of the LORD. Judges 4:1

Ehud was an anointed judge raised up by God from the tribe of Benjamin. Ehud killed the obese Moabite king Eglon with a knife (see Judges 3). Moab was created from the incestuous union of Lot and his oldest daughter. Lot became extremely drunk with wine at the hand of his daughters and they lay with him to procreate. Lot was so drunk he did not know when they came in or left him. Moab means "seed of the father" and inherited the curses of Sodom that had just been destroyed. Moabites tended to bring great immorality and sensuality into the land. Eglon was a fat man consumed with personal pleasures. His belly was his god. Because of Israel's rebellion against the word of God, Eglon was enabled to take over the trade routes through the Jordan River, and he controlled the best parts of the Jordan river valley. He subjected Israel to oppression for eighteen years.

Ehud was raised up to deliver Israel. Ehud's name means, "Joined together; strong; union. He that praises." Ehud today represents holy unity in the body of Christ to overthrow sensuality and toleration for lewdness. Ehud's victory was so great that the land came into peace for eighty years. When Ehud died, the Israelites quickly went back to idolatry.

When holiness and unity in the body of Christ is destroyed, the people of God are not strong enough to stand against the assaults of Satan. When carnality and disunity compromise a Christian marriage, the children are often taken captive by the world system as selfish parents cannot operate in righteous dominion and pray off all of Satan's assaults.

When Ehud was dead, the holiness and unity of Israel shattered and every man began to do what he felt was right in his own eyes. They lived by soul realm and natural reason rather than revelation and relationship. Rather than looking to God's word for the standard of measure for righteousness, people began deciding their own standard of measure. This constitutes eating from the tree of the knowledge of good and evil. Wanting to become like God, the people established their own code of ethics and they decided what was good and what was evil. This happens by intellectualism and natural reason and is a form of humanism, the exaltation of man's reason to a place of divine revelation. God hates to see this happen and releases judgment to bring man back into line.

Jabin, King of Canaan

So the LORD sold them into the hand of Jabin king of Canaan, who reigned in Hazor. The commander of his army was Sisera, who dwelt in Harosheth Hagoyim. And the children of Israel cried out to the LORD; for Jabin had nine hundred chariots of iron, and for twenty years he harshly oppressed the children of Israel. Judges 4:2-3

God's people broke from unity in following God's voice and began to do evil. The Bible says that the Lord **"sold them into the hand of Jabin king of Canaan."** This is an extremely harsh word. God sold them into slavery. When we reject God's word and do evil by practicing unrighteousness, we become the slaves of sin. Jabin is a terrible ruler who represents a dark spirit that assaults the Church today. He harshly oppressed the children of Israel and made life miserable for them.

Jabin's name means "God discerns; he will understand; whom He considered; He that understands, intelligent." Jabin represents intellectual pride and religion similar to the Pharisees of Jesus' day. The religious leader who talks about God from an unanointed intellectual perspective builds strongholds in the minds of his followers so as to control them and deceive them to doctrines of demons. Jabin is a picture of Satan, the father of lies who creates all the religions of the world to deceive God's creatures. Satan counterfeits true Christianity with false doctrines. Satan hates the Church and when the Church is in compromise and mixture, he often is able to harshly oppress believers.

Soul realm living as a "Christian" is a religion rooted in fear that walks by "sight." God calls us to walk by faith in His revealed rhema word (voice). Intellectualism operates by man's interpretation of the Bible rather than God's voice heard through intimate communion gained through praise, worship, prayer, meditation and waiting on the anointing. An intellectual, reason oriented approach to understanding the Bible can only lead to a life rooted in fear seeking to control to find a sense of peace and security. It is a futile endeavor. One can only find rest by taking the yoke of Jesus and walking in perfect agreement with Him by an intimate relationship with the Holy Spirit (Matthew 11:28-30). The spirit that Jabin represents attempts to rule churches through intelligent, strong, talented and skilled "Christian" leaders. He has far more influence in American churches than most realize.

Jabin's name means "he will understand." Pastors and Christian counselors can get into a compromising spirit about sin and declare, "God understands your struggle. He loves you and is a God of grace. He knows you are trying to follow Him and He forgives you." The believer can be led to rationalize all manners of sin in this way including lust, fantasy, pornography, self-indulgent entertainment, gluttony, adultery, rage, abusive behavior, stubbornness, bitterness, laziness and pride. Some pastors have a "boys will be boys" attitude that condones men's immoral behavior. Jabin teaches a "cheap grace" theology that gets into agreement with man's pride. Jabin rationalizes to the carnal mind that God understands your struggle and that God is not angry that we tolerate sexual perversions and demonized behavior in our lives. Jabin is a wicked liar. God hates sin and wants to deliver us from tolerating sin in our lives!

Jabin was also the King of Canaan. Canaan means,

"Merchants, trader, a trafficker, to bring down low into subjection; to humiliate; humble." Merchants and trading speaks to us of bringing worldly merchandising into the house of God. It speaks to us of running the Church like a business. When man starts running church like a business, the King of Canaan comes in to humiliate us, to bring us low into subjection. We are humiliated by our carnality and powerlessness over sin, sickness and disease. Jesus drove out the merchandisers from the temple who polluted it with their filthy money loving ways. Jabin controlled the land for his personal profit just as Satan tries to control churches through deceived pastors.

The American business model powerfully influences most American churches. Most churches are consumer oriented. They provide goods and services to a target market in return for tithes, offerings and volunteer work. Many churches are designed to meet the needs of the "Christian" consumer. Facilities, programs and activities are all geared towards meeting the needs of a cultural Christian public.

Some churches extend their influence over many other like-minded churches and develop a franchise approach with a common name. There is often carnal competition with other franchise churches in the region to attract the customers from the Christian cultural target market. Better facilities, programs, music and activities delivered in one location can often cause people to change churches. The Christian public tends to shop around to find a church "where their needs are being met." Rather than listen to the Holy Spirit direct them where they should go to worship God and serve Him, the consumer looks for where her needs are met and where she feels most comfortable.

The spirit of Jabin rules the business model church with its carnal programs, five-year goals and fleshly church growth strategies. God hates it and will bring it down through anointed Deborahs of the last days. Jabin was a king who ruled in the Promised Land of Canaan after Joshua's conquest. What's wrong with this picture? God's people were supposed to hold that land, but they couldn't because they came under the intellectual merchandising spirit and did what was right in their own natural minds!

Canaan was the cursed son of Ham who mocked Noah's nakedness (Genesis 9:25) and prophetically seeks to humiliate God's people and control their land. The spirit behind Canaan exposes people's nakedness and mocks the "little people" who are not strong enough to make it. This is a faultfinding spirit and accuser of the brethren.

The entire land of Israel was called Canaan. Jabin, the king of Canaan is a reference to Satan who tries to prevent us from taking possession of our Promised Land. He seeks to keep us out of our inheritance, which is to walk as Jesus walked in perfect love, holiness and power. He seeks to steal our birthright so that we do not achieve our destiny or bear fruit unto God.

Jabin reigned in Hazor, which was about 10 miles north of the Sea of Galilee. Hazor means, "Fence, castle, a court; to trumpet; enclosure." The king of Canaan seeks to control business, government, church and homes through soulish men. He wants to box the people of God into His castle and enclose them in traditions and programs that come from man's ideas and not God's revelation.

The ancient King of Hazor controlled all political alliances in the land (see Joshua 11:1-15). This spirit knows how to bring power politics into the house of God especially through denominationalism, old traditions and respectability. He uses the false spiritual authority of witchcraft that manifests in manipulation, flattery, intimidation and domination to control followers. This king ultimately seeks to build a throne for himself where he can be the center of attention, focus and worship. He finds access to rule those who are independent and self-focused. He deceives those whose hidden ambitions are to achieve fame, fortune and recognition. He has a powerful influence on male pastors who rely on their intelligence, skill, personality and hard work to run the church. These men have great talent and work hard but inwardly they are very insecure because they measure themselves by their performance and achievements rather than by an intimate relationship with Jesus. As a result, they seek the approval of man and get caught in a snare of trying to please the people rather than fearing the Lord and obeying His voice.

Jabin created a war machine that included nine hundred chariots of iron that maintained his evil rule over God's people. Chariots speak to us of vehicles of transportation. Nine is the number of the gifts of the Holy Spirit. Jabin works his control through extremely talented and competent individuals who are highly gifted. Iron speaks of earthly strength and hardness of heart. Most Christian leaders are extremely talented individuals who work hard. They can learn sacrifice instead of mercy and easily become the Pharisees of our day. Jabin rules through these chariot drivers who know how to make things happen and get things done in the house of God.

"Unless the LORD builds the house, they labor in vain who build it; unless the LORD guards the city, the watchman stays awake in vain" (Psalm 127:1). The Lord does not build His house in the way of Jabin. God uses chariots of fire refined by the seven fires of the Holy Spirit. God uses humble broken vessels who operate by the leading of the Holy Spirit, not by natural reason or intellectual persuasion. God's true leaders do not operate by authority mixed with witchcraft that always seeks to build a throne for man's glory, but rather they operate in spiritual authority that leads with love, servanthood and the manifestations of holy power seen in healing, deliverance and salvations.

Jabin had 900 chariots and thousands of foot soldiers. We can see that several denominations have more than 900 churches and many have become religious chariots of iron that possess the land of God's people with unrighteous control. God is going to deliver many churches from Jabin by the hand of a woman who operates solely by the Spirit of God in true prophetic anointing. Anointed intercessors who learn to pray by the Spirit will confound the wisdom of men and bring down the rule of the sons of Greece who run the church by intellectual pride and soul realm works of their own hands (see Zechariah 9:13).

General Sisera

The commander of his army was Sisera, who dwelt in Harosheth Hagoyim. And the children of Israel cried out to the LORD; for Jabin had nine hundred chariots of iron, and for twenty years he harshly oppressed the children of Israel. Judges 4:2,3

With every dragon, there is a beast, the antichrist and his false prophet, the king and his general. Behind every highly visible leader is a practical man who manages the operation. Jabin was the visionary leader, the king of Canaan. He relied upon Sisera to make it all happen. Jabin represents Satan and Sisera the leader in the natural realm through whom he works his evil.

Sisera's name means, "A crane of seeing. A field of battle; sea of horses, meditation; to leap onward; to make an onset. Binding in chains. Found on a horse." Sisera, chief general of Jabin, represents an evil demonic spirit who seeks to rule churches with iron chariots (programs) and binds carnal men in chains so that they work with their hands apart from the Holy Spirit. Sisera represents a skillful leader who can make things happen and get things done. He wants to leap onward and build a big ministry. He is found on the horse of domination and control. He is overwhelmingly powerful in accomplishments because of his strong personality and talents so that he can keep 900 chariot drivers moving. He feels great satisfaction in making progress and getting things done. He is a great administrator and knows how to facilitate the smooth operation of the business of churches without the help of the Holy Spirit. He is influenced by a devil! Beware of his spirit in the house of God.

Sisera dwelt in Harosheth Hagoyim. Harosheth means "Manufacturing; engraving, stone, wood and iron works; to keep silent; to plow." Hagoyim means "A foreign nation; Gentile; a troop of animals (demons), or a flight of locusts, heathen peoples." The Lord is giving us clues as to who this spirit is, how he works and where he lives. Sisera lives in a place of manufacturing, a place of getting things done. He wants his workers to keep silent and keep plowing for his benefit. He lives in Hagoyim, which represents the lost people of the earth. His demons are around the world enslaving people to hard oppressive work with little or no hope to break out of poverty.

The vast majority of the seven billion residents of the earth are in slavery to Satan and are under his oppressive rule. The majority of North American churches have become subject in some measure to this worldly spirit and are ineffective in reaching out to lost nations, let alone changing the moral free fall of our own land. Israel was in bondage to Satan in a similar fashion and God raised up and anointed a woman to deliver the people and bring down the oppressors. God is going to do it again!

God chose a prophetic woman to come against the intellectual compromising spirit of Jabin and Sisera. Deborah was an intercessor with an intimate relationship with her God. She heard God's voice and obeyed Him. God looked for an intercessor to stand in the gap for Israel. He found Deborah crying out to Him in desperate prevailing prayer for several years. At the proper time, the Lord exalted her to be the judge over the nation and deliver the people, who cried out to God, for deliverance from Jabin and Sisera.

CHAPTER 7

DEBORAH, THE PROPHET AND JUDGE

Now Deborah, a prophetess, the wife of Lapidoth, was judging Israel at that time. And she would sit under the palm tree of Deborah between Ramah and Bethel in the mountains of Ephraim. And the children of Israel came up to her for judgment. Then she sent and called for Barak the son of Abinoam from Kedesh in Naphtali, and said to him, "Has not the LORD God of Israel commanded, 'Go and deploy troops at Mount Tabor; take with you ten thousand men of the sons of Naphtali and of the sons of Zebulun; and against you I will deploy Sisera, the commander of Jabin's army, with his chariots and his multitude at the River Kishon; and I will deliver him into your hand'?" And Barak said to her, "If you will go with me, then I will go; but if you will not go with me, I will not go!" So she said, "I will surely go with you; nevertheless there will be no glory for you in the journey you are taking, for the LORD will sell Sisera into the hand of a woman." Then Deborah arose and went with Barak to Kedesh. And Barak called Zebulun and Naphtali to

Kedesh; he went up with ten thousand men under his command, and Deborah went up with him. Judges 4:4-10

After the children of Israel suffered twenty years of oppression by Jabin and Sisera, God raised up the powerfully anointed leader named Deborah. She sat, as a symbol of her great authority, under the palm tree between Ramah and Bethel, in the mountains of Ephraim. Every detail was given to instruct us in the way of the Holy Spirit.

Deborah is the fourth judge of Israel. Some scholars list Barak as the fourth judge and name Deborah as the fifth. While Barak was a great general who is honored in Hebrews 11:32, the Bible does not declare that he was a judge. Placing Barak as a judge ahead of Deborah may be another example of gender bias. Deborah was the anointed judge over the nation and she was the inspirational leader of the people.

Deborah is a prophetic picture of the last-day five-fold prophetic warrior bride. She represents the prophetic voice of women in ministry including five-fold offices. Deborah means, "Eloquent; an orator; bee; from the root meaning to speak, her speaking." The name Deborah represents a prophetic voice that declares the oracles of God. A prophet is the mouthpiece of God and must represent Him faithfully to the people. The bee represents the prophetic person who takes flight into the spiritual realm to gather the honey of God's word and the impartation of His anointing. Deborahs are led by the Spirit to go to conferences and churches in various places to receive impartation and equipping. They will travel over land and sea to gather the nectar of the Holy Spirit's anointing.

The bee packs a powerful stinger as a weapon. The stinger represents the piercing and judgment aspects of God's word and the power of spiritual warfare. The word of God is the sword of the Spirit and is like a fire, hammer and battle-ax in the mouth of an anointed prophet. Only those who walk by the Spirit can wield this weapon like a mighty stinger that it is.

Deborah's husband was named Lapidoth which means, "Torches, having eyes of fire; enlightened; lighting flashes; from a root meaning a torch, a lamp, to flame, to shine, flames." Lapidoth is a picture of the heavenly bridegroom, the Lord Jesus Christ, with eyes a flame of fire. Eyes of fire represent Jesus' passionate, zealous desire for His prophetic warrior bride. Flashes of lightning represent His powerful revelations and judgments that come from His throne. The face of the risen Christ is bright like lightning, and He has the power of lightning hidden in His hands (Revelation 1:16; Habakuk 3:4). A flash flood overwhelmed Sisera and his 900 chariots that was accompanied by flashes of lightning (see Judges 5:4,5,20,21).

Deborah's Dwelling Place

And she would sit under the palm tree of Deborah between Ramah and Bethel in the mountains of Ephraim. And the children of Israel came up to her for judgment. Judges 4:5

Deborah dwelt between Ramah and Bethel in the mountains of Ephraim. Ramah means, "High place dedicated to idols," and represents the foolish pride and vanity of man who turns from God to create his own gods. Bethel means, "The house of God," and represents the true place where God dwells. Deborah was called to judge between Ramah, man's idolatrous pride, and Bethel, the standards of God's house revealed in His holy word.

Deborah was of the tribe of Ephraim and judged God's people in the mountains of Ephraim. Joseph's second son born in Egypt during a time of bountiful harvest was named

Ephraim. Ephraim represents the second-generation prophets blessed of God. Ephraim means, "Two fold increase; very fruitful; doubly fruitful." Deborah was a prophet who dwelt in the "mountains of Ephraim." She lived a life of fruitfulness because she embraced the prophetic revelation from God's throne as she sat under a palm tree.

The children of Israel came to this mother in Israel because she had the anointing of God over the nation as a judge and spoke the words of truth. Deborah was given authority by God to lead the nation in matters of God's holy Law and all the people recognized it. No one opposed Deborah simply because she was a woman. To oppose Deborah would have been to oppose God and His anointing.

The Palm Tree of Deborah

Deborah sat under the palm tree of Deborah and judged Israel. The fact that Deborah sat is a picture of authority and judgment. Deborah sat under a palm tree as a prophetic intercessor between Heaven and Earth. She was a door through which God revealed His voice to the people. The palm tree also represents the prophetic voice of the Holy Spirit.

Palm trees were carved on the doors of Solomon's temple representing that God flows the wind of His Spirit through redeemed human vessels, covered with the anointing of gold, His divine nature. The temple door represents an entry point from the natural to the spiritual realm. As the priest entered through the temple door, it was a picture of going from the natural realm into the presence of God in the third heaven. Deborah sat at a spiritual door and judged tribes. She became a vessel through whom God spoke from Heaven to Earth to lead His people. Deborah received throne room revelation from above and gave it to men on Earth (see also Deuteronomy 16:18; 17:9-12).

The deep roots of palm trees speak of our humanity. The ability of palm trees to bend in the wind speaks of the ability of the prophet to flow with the Holy Spirit in all things. The branches at the top represent the divine, victorious life where all good fruit is born by the wind of the Spirit.

Palm branches were waved at Jesus' triumphal entry. They are a sign of the entrance of the King into the land. Palm trees represent the righteous triumph at the end of the age by victorious saints who have conformed to the image of Jesus (see Revelation 7:9). The Feast of Tabernacles included palm branches, a sign that Jesus will tabernacle among us and help us overcome. God wants to tabernacle in our hearts since we are now the temples of the Holy Spirit.

The palm tree is a picture of ascending unto the mountain of Zion to experience revelation from God while still rooted in the practical realities of natural realm living. Palm trees were found throughout Solomon's temple. They also picture the warm climate of God's love by the seashore. God wants His love to go out to the sea of humanity with warmth and triumph so that He can tabernacle among them.

God is looking for Deborahs to dwell in the mountains of Ephraim and live by God's fruit bearing prophetic voice. He will give them a place of authority to be a door through which God can flow His revelation to judge between what is of man's pride and what is of God's house. God will raise up many in this hour.

General Barak

Then she sent and called for Barak the son of Abinoam from Kedesh in Naphtali. Judges 4:6a

Barak was a man who responded to Deborah's call. He submitted to her leadership and desired her presence in the final battle because God was with her. Barak is a partial

129

picture of the warrior King Jesus. Barak would not go up to battle without Deborah, just as Jesus will not conquer His enemies without His last-day warrior bride. Barak means, "Lightning; thunder; thunderbolt." Barak represents the powerful intervention of Jesus that comes like lightning to defeat His enemies. Jesus Christ is the King of Kings and the Lord of hosts. He is the great military Ruler who conquers all His enemies. He is waiting for His bride to mature as Deborah because He will not go out to conquer in the end time without her.

Barak was the son of Abinoam whose name means, "Father of pleasantness; father of beauty, father of grace." Abinoam is a picture of the heavenly Father who sent His Son to conquer sin and death. Abinoam came from Kedesh in Naphtali. Kedesh means, "Sanctuary; holy place from the root meaning to consecrate." The Father lives in the Holy Place in heaven and sets apart His people. Abinoam was from Naphtali, who along with Zebulun, were the two primary tribes chosen to overcome the enemies of God.

The Prophetic Meaning of Naphtali

And Rachel's maid Bilhah conceived again and bore Jacob a second son. Then Rachel said, "With great wrestlings I have wrestled with my sister, and indeed I have prevailed." So she called his name Naphtali. Genesis 30:7,8

Naphtali means "a struggle; my wrestling; my twisting; obtained by wrestling." Naphtali is the twelfth and final gate on the western wall of Zion (Ezekiel 48:34). We are to go through the gates of Zion and prepare a way for the people to come in (Isaiah 62:10). Going through the gates of Naphtali and Zebulun enable us to reach the last-day harvest.

Naphtali is the twelfth gate. Twelve speaks of apostolic

government and west speaks of the end of the age. We need the restoration of God's five-fold apostolic government at the end of the age. This will include many women ministers.

Naphtali was the sixth born son of Jacob and the second born of Bilhah, who previously gave birth to Dan. Six is the number of man, and Naphtali represents the conclusion of the efforts of man through the ages to wrestle with God and obtain His blessings as Jacob once did. We wrestle through prevailing prayer and faithful obedience with patient endurance. We also have to wrestle in the Spirit against **"principalities, against powers, against the rulers of the darkness of this age, against spiritual hosts of wickedness in the heavenly places" (Ephesians 6:12b)** to bind the strongman and loose souls to receive the word of salvation.

"Naphtali is a deer let loose; he uses beautiful words" (Genesis 49:21). Jacob prophesied the anointing over the tribe of Naphtali as an evangelist. Ancient Hebrew literature states that Naphtali outran his brothers to tell Jacob the glad tidings that Joseph was alive in Egypt. Naphtali rejoices in the true prophetic. Jacob declared that Naphtali would have a free spirit and would speak beautiful words. Naphtali pictures a last-day Church that is let loose to run with the Spirit declaring the good news to bring in the final worldwide harvest.

And of Naphtali he said: "O Naphtali, satisfied with favor, and full of the blessing of the LORD, possess the west and the south." Deuteronomy 33:23

Moses prophetically blessed Naphtali to be satisfied with favor and full of the blessing of the Lord, which speaks of the complete fulfillment of the blessings of Israel and the Church in the final days. Moses declared that Naphtali would possess the west and the south. In the natural, Naphtali possessed the western bank of the sea of Galilee and some of the best portions of all the land of Israel. West speaks to us of the end of the day and south speaks to us of the warm blessings of summer. God saves the best wine for last as Naphtali will experience.

We must go through the gate of Naphtali by wrestling with God to obtain the revelation of His favor. We must also wrestle against all resistance so that we can take the kingdom of heaven by violent action (Matthew 11:12). Then He will birth the last-day moves of His Spirit through us. This will include the greatest evangelistic harvest of all times. The deer let loose speaks to us of an energetic, joyful missionary adventure where anointed sent ones go skipping and leaping on hills with Jesus to win nations for His glory. This is also prophetically pictured in Jesus' first coming.

And leaving Nazareth, He came and dwelt in Capernaum, which is by the sea, in the regions of Zebulun and Naphtali, that it might be fulfilled which was spoken by Isaiah the prophet, saying: "The land of Zebulun and the land of Naphtali, by the way of the sea, beyond the Jordan, Galilee of the Gentiles: The people who sat in darkness have seen a great light, and upon those who sat in the region and shadow of death Light has dawned."

From that time Jesus began to preach and to say, "Repent, for the kingdom of heaven is at hand." And Jesus, walking by the Sea of Galilee, saw two brothers, Simon called Peter, and Andrew his brother, casting a net into the sea; for they were fishermen. Then He said to them, "Follow Me, and I will make you fishers of men." They immediately left their nets and followed Him. Going on from there, He saw two other brothers, James the son of Zebedee, and John his brother, in the boat with Zebedee their father, mending their nets. And He called them, and immediately they left the boat and their father, and followed Him. Matthew 4:13-22

After Jesus' initial message in Nazareth was rejected, He came and dwelt in the region of Zebulun and Naphtali by the sea of Galilee **"of the Gentiles."** The great light Jesus revealed was to go to all the world. He chose fishermen including Peter, Andrew, James and John from this region and made them great evangelist–apostles as He birthed the Church by His blood and the power of His resurrection life.

It is fitting that the last gate of Zion portray the heart of Jesus to send an evangelistic, apostolic company to take a great harvest of fish from the sea. We go through the gate of Naphtali by accepting the challenge to go to all the world with the gospel of Jesus Christ. God will use many young energetic bucks and does and loose them to the nations with the glad tidings as He did with His first disciples.

Abinoam, the father of Barak, was from Naphtali. The heart of our heavenly Father longs for the evangelistic harvest of the nations. The tribe of Naphtali was chosen in the story of Deborah because they were in agreement with Barak, who came from that tribe. Jesus chose disciples from the region of Naphtali who had the pure heart of evangelism to reach the world. As the Church of Deborah arises, the greatest evangelistic harvest of all times will begin. Zebulun was also chosen to war with Naphtali in this battle against Jabin and Sisera.

The Prophetic Meaning of Zebulun

Then Leah conceived again and bore Jacob a sixth son. And Leah said, "God has endowed me with a good endowment; now my husband will dwell with me, because I have borne him six sons." So she called his name Zebulun. Genesis 30:19-20

Leah longed to be loved by Jacob and have his affections. When she bore him a sixth son, the tenth son overall, she named him Zebulun declaring her longing to dwell with her husband. Zebulun means "Wished for habitation; dwelling; to dwell with." There is a longing heart in the anointing of Zebulun to dwell with Jesus, the heavenly Bridegroom. Zebulun represents intense longing for intimacy with Jesus. We go through the gate of Zebulun by pursuing an intimate relationship with Jesus so we can hear and obey His voice only. As tenth born, Zebulun reminds us of the ten plagues and the ten commandments. God releases judgment on those who break His laws.

Zebulun is the ninth gate on the south wall of the city of Zion (Ezekiel 48:33). There are nine gifts of the Holy Spirit and nine fruits of the Spirit. Those who are intimate with Jesus will bear the fruit of His character and receive the gifts of His Spirit and operate in them. South represents the warmth of summer and the favor of God during a season of growing. Those who experience intimacy in the light of the King's face will have His favor (Proverbs 16:15).

"Zebulun shall dwell by the haven of the sea; he shall become a haven for ships, and his border shall adjoin Sidon" (Genesis 49:13). Zebulun's land bordered the Kishon river that flowed into the Mediterranean Sea. Jacob prophesied that Zebulun would be a haven of ships. This speaks of supporting apostolic ministries, providing a safe harbor for those who come and go, doing the work of evangelism. The tribe of Zebulun included those who fished in the sea as a picture of their heart for evangelism. The sea represents the nations of the world. As we dwell with Jesus in intimacy He imparts His heart for the nations to us. This motivates missionaries to go out and catch a great harvest of souls from the sea of the nations. People shall also come from nations to those who have provided a habitation for the Lord so they may experience His presence.

And of Zebulun he said: "Rejoice, Zebulun, in your going out, and Issachar in your tents! They shall call the peoples to the mountain; there they shall offer sacrifices of righteousness; for they shall partake of the abundance of the seas and of treasures hidden in the sand."

Deuteronomy 33:18-19

Entering the gate of Zebulun, the habitation of God, requires righteous and holy living. Those who walk in holiness and intimacy partake of the abundance of the harvest of souls in the nations. They discover natural and spiritual treasures in their relationship with Jesus Christ **"in whom are hidden all the treasures of wisdom and knowledge" (Colossians 2:3).** They will also have abundant resources to finance the last great harvest.

In Deborah's prophetic song, she prophesied, **"And from Zebulun those who bear the recruiter's staff"** and **"Zebulun is a people who jeopardized their lives to the point of death" (Judges 5:14,18).** Zebulun speaks of evangelists who recruit new souls for the army of God. As bold evangelists, they risk their lives to serve the Lord in the dangerous places of foreign nations.

Zebulun may have also recruited the neighboring tribe of Issachar who apparently joined the battle once engaged (Judges 5:15). Issachar means "he brings wages, rewarded" and had an anointing to know the times and seasons (I Chronicles 12:32). They were wise to join in the battle and reap the rewards of the spoils as Moses prophesied (Deuteronomy 33:18,19).

The tribes of Zebulun and Naphtali warred in perfect agreement with Issachar to help Deborah and Barak defeat the armies of Sisera. This pictures a powerful end time warfare of agreement among evangelists to reach the lost in the world. It is a powerful warfare between the kingdom of God (Barak and Deborah – Jesus and His Bride) and the kingdom of darkness (Jabin and Sisera – Satan and false prophets).

Jesus recruited most of His apostles from the area of Zebulun and Naphtali including Peter, Andrew, James and John. They became the pillars of the Church for the move of the Holy Spirit and great evangelism. The result of the evangelism seen in the book of Acts was a great harvest of souls from the seas of this world. This was a first-fruits harvest. The Lord has planned a much greater harvest of souls for the end of the age.

We raise up the banner of Zebulun by seeking to be intimate with the Lord and allowing Him to dwell in our midst and rule our lives. In His presence, there is fullness of joy and peace. Being close to the King, our hearts will become one, and we will begin to see that the lost in the world are white unto harvest. We must go through the gate of Zebulun and become recruiters for the army of God through evangelism as Jesus' first-century disciples did.

The Prophetic Word to Barak

Then she sent and called for Barak the son of Abinoam from Kedesh in Naphtali, and said to him, "Has not the LORD God of Israel commanded, 'Go and deploy troops at Mount Tabor; take with you ten thousand men of the sons of Naphtali and of the sons of Zebulun; and against you I will deploy Sisera, the commander of Jabin's army, with his chariots and his multitude at the River Kishon; and I will deliver him into your hand'?" Judges 4:6,7

Deborah sent one of her associates from Ephraim to Kedesh, a distance of ninety miles, to call Barak to her. This is a sign of Deborah's incredible authority. Barak responded to the associate's call and came to present himself before the anointed judge of the nation. Barak listened with respect and honor as Deborah told him the directive prophetic word of the Lord to go into battle against Sisera.

Barak must have had complete confidence that this was the word of the Lord because Sisera had 900 chariots and had undoubtedly defeated Israel's resistance before. Also the armies of Israel had no swords or spears (see Judges 5:8). Deborah gave Barak the strategy of the Lord with the instructions to deploy troops at Mount Tabor and to take 10,000 men from the tribes of Naphtali and Zebulun. The Lord declared through Deborah that He would deliver Jabin's army and his chariots into Barak's hand at the River Kishon.

Tabor means "You will purge; stone quarry; separated, height, purity." Tabor represents the authority and anointing of believers separated unto God and fashioned as living stones. Tabor was a strategic domed mountain on the borders of Zebulun and Naphtali (Joshua 19:22). It was often fortified for wars and was a perfect staging area for the battle. Nazareth was less than six miles northwest and Jesus would have hiked to the top of Tabor many times during His life on Earth to pray.

Jerome and other Church fathers believed Tabor was the mountain of transfiguration where Moses and Elijah appeared to the radiant Lord Jesus Christ (Matthew 17:1-8). That view fits an end time prophetic picture of the rapture and return of the bride transfigured with Christ from the heights of heaven, riding on white horses to conquer the enemies of God that gather against Him (see Revelation 19:11-16).

God's people must enter into the presence of the Lord and behold Him in His glory so they can be transformed to become like Him (II Corinthians 3:18). We must assemble at Mount Tabor in the Spirit and be fashioned as quarried stones of the temple to fit into our place in the holy temple God is building. We are called to come out of Babylon and be separated unto the Lord so that we can be useful in His service.

The kings came and fought, then the kings of Canaan fought in Taanach, by the waters of Megiddo; they took no spoils of silver. They fought from the heavens; the stars from their courses fought against Sisera.

137

The torrent of Kishon swept them away, that ancient torrent, the torrent of Kishon. O my soul, march on in strength! Judges 5:19-21

Deborah's song tells us that God sent a torrent of rain from the heavens and the flash flood swept through the Kishon river and wiped out the Canaanite armies that fought in Taanach by the waters of Megiddo.

Kishon means "Torturer; winding about; ensnarer," and represents demonic traps and spiritual warfare from Satan. The evil armies of Sisera and Jabin seek to trap people in sin and bring them into everlasting torment with them. Kishon represents the place of judgment for evil workers. Elijah killed the false prophets of Baal here (I Kings 18:40). God is raising up Deborahs who will bring God's flood against false prophets.

Taanach means "She will afflict you; wandering through; castle; sandy soil." The enemy certainly wants to afflict God's people and cause them to wander, especially in their carnal minds. Those who walk in opposition to the kingdom of God build stronghold castles in their minds on sandy soil rather than the rock of inspired revelation. They will not stand in the judgment of God.

Meggido means "Place of troops; place of multitudes; from the root to crowd in great numbers in one place." Meggido also means, "Invading; gathering for cutting (self); his cutting-place." Armageddon is a compound name meaning "the mountain of Meggido." The city of Meggido became a symbol of the meeting place for the last-day conflict between God and all His enemies (see Revelation 16:16). The general area where Jabin's troops were defeated by the power of God is a prophetic picture of God's wrath poured out at the end of the age against all the armies of the nations who gather against the Lord and His anointed One (see Psalm 2).

If You Will Go With Me, Then I Will Go

And Barak said to her, "If you will go with me, then I will go; but if you will not go with me, I will not go!" So she said, "I will surely go with you; nevertheless there will be no glory for you in the journey you are taking, for the LORD will sell Sisera into the hand of a woman." Then Deborah arose and went with Barak to Kedesh. And Barak called Zebulun and Naphtali to Kedesh; he went up with ten thousand men under his command, and Deborah went up with him. Judges 4:8-10

Barak recognized the tremendous anointing on Deborah and exclaimed, by the Spirit, the heart of Jesus towards His warrior bride: **"If you will go with me, then I will go; but if you will not go with me, I will not go!"** The King of Kings does not come riding from heaven alone in the last battle. He brings His ten thousands of saints who ride with Him on white horses. He will not conquer Satan without His bride at His side.

Now I saw heaven opened, and behold, a white horse. And He who sat on him was called Faithful and True, and in righteousness He judges and makes war. His eyes were like a flame of fire, and on His head were many crowns. He had a name written that no one knew except Himself. He was clothed with a robe dipped in blood, and His name is called The Word of God. <u>And the armies in heaven, clothed in fine linen, white and clean, followed Him on white horses</u>. Now out of His mouth goes a sharp sword, that with it He should strike the nations. And He Himself will rule them with a rod of iron. He Himself treads the winepress of the fierceness and wrath of Almighty God. And He has on His robe and on His thigh a name written: KING OF KINGS AND LORD OF LORDS. Revelation 19:11-16 (underlining mine)

Years ago during a powerful worship service in Tijuana, Mexico where I was ministering, I had a vision of Jesus riding into the sanctuary on an enormous white horse. His robe was completely bright red and His eyes twinkled with fiery life. He winked at me and said, "Do you want to come ride with Me and win some nations?" My heart pounded as I enthusiastically replied in my heart, "Yes Lord, I'll ride with You!" For years the Church has sung the song with that famous line. Those who hear the prophetic voice of God will rise up and ride with Jesus in a wave of last-day evangelism.

Ten Thousands of His Saints

Now Enoch, the seventh from Adam, prophesied about these men also, saying, "Behold, the Lord comes with ten thousands of His saints, to execute judgment on all, to convict all who are ungodly among them of all their ungodly deeds which they have committed in an ungodly way, and of all the harsh things which ungodly sinners have spoken against Him." Jude 14,15

Barak and Deborah led ten thousands of God's saints into battle against Jabin's army headed by Sisera. The Spirit led them to do this as a prophetic picture of the judgment of the ungodly at the end of the age. Ten thousands is a complete number and is used a number of times in Scripture to express a complete large number (see also Genesis 24:60; Deuteronomy 33:2,17; I Samuel 18:7,8; Psalm 3:6).

At the end of the age, ten thousands of God's saints will return and ride with Jesus to execute judgment and to reign and rule with Him. Deborah was called to be at the side of Barak. He would not go to battle without her. The warrior bride must ride with Jesus. The Lord will honor women who take their place in the battle. Women must take their place in ministry so that the explosive last-day harvest can truly begin!

CHAPTER 8

DEBORAH, THE WARRIOR

Now Heber the Kenite, of the children of Hobab the father-in-law of Moses, had separated himself from the Kenites and pitched his tent near the terebinth tree at Zaanaim, which is beside Kedesh. And they reported to Sisera that Barak the son of Abinoam had gone up to Mount Tabor. So Sisera gathered together all his chariots, nine hundred chariots of iron, and all the people who were with him, from Harosheth Hagoyim to the River Kishon. Then Deborah said to Barak, "Up! For this is the day in which the LORD has delivered Sisera into your hand. Has not the LORD gone out before you?" So Barak went down from Mount Tabor with ten thousand men following him. And the LORD routed Sisera and all his chariots and all his army with the edge of the sword before Barak; and Sisera alighted from his chariot and fled away on foot. But Barak pursued the chariots and the army as far as Harosheth Hagoyim, and all the army of Sisera fell by the edge of the sword; not a man was left.

However, Sisera had fled away on foot to the tent of Jael, the wife of Heber the Kenite; for there was peace between Jabin king of Hazor and the house of Heber the Kenite. And Jael went out to meet Sisera, and said to him, "Turn aside, my lord, turn aside to me; do not fear." And when he had turned aside with her into the tent, she covered him with a blanket. Then he said to her, "Please give me a little water to drink, for I am thirsty." So she opened a jug of milk, gave him a drink, and covered him. And he said to her, "Stand at the door of the tent, and if any man comes and inquires of you, and says, 'Is there any man here?' you shall say, 'No.'" Then Jael, Heber's wife, took a tent peg and took a hammer in her hand, and went softly to him and drove the peg into his temple, and it went down into the ground; for he was fast asleep and weary. So he died. And then, as Barak pursued Sisera, Jael came out to meet him, and said to him, "Come, I will show you the man whom you seek." And when he went into her tent, there lay Sisera, dead with the peg in his temple.

So on that day God subdued Jabin king of Canaan in the presence of the children of Israel. And the hand of the children of Israel grew stronger and stronger against Jabin king of Canaan, until they had destroyed Jabin king of Canaan. Judges 4:11-24

The war to deliver Israel from their oppressors was completely guided by the sovereign hand of the Most High God. As Barak gathered his troops from as far north as Kadesh, Heber, a prominent man in the neighboring city of Zaanaim, observed the troop movements and reported them to Sisera, some 40 miles southwest in Harosheth on the Kishon River.

Heber's name means, "Community; companion from the root, a society; also a spell; charmer, enchantment." Heber was a Kenite, a name which means, "A nest; or resting place in a high rock." Heber was a descendant of Hobab whom the text declares was the father-in-law of Moses who lived some 300 years prior. Heber was a rugged individualist who separated his family from his ancestral roots of Midian to the south and from fellow Kenites in the region.

Heber's name and actions indicate that he was a charming man who knew how to play power politics and get along with the rulers of his day. He was always looking to build his nest in the high places of society. Heber had made deals with Sisera and Jabin so that he could live in peace and prosperity. As such, he sold his soul to the devil. Heber came under the enchantment of the enemy and became a spy for him hoping for some benefit.

Heber represents an independent man with high prominence and position who operates in soul power and personality and makes compromises for personal gain. He was a strong man who carved out a small place in history for himself as a carnal fool. God probably used Heber's hardness of heart to train his wife Jael as Saul was used to train David.

Heber's information launched Sisera into action with his 900 chariots of iron and thousands of foot soldiers who gathered in the valley of Jezreel southwest of Mount Tabor. The 900 chariots of iron would have served like powerful Sherman tanks to offset the descending infantry of Naphtali, Zebulun and some of Issachar who joined the battle. History records that hailstones fell from heaven in addition to the torrent of Kishon created by the flash flood.

The chariots of iron quickly became mired in the sandy soil of Taanach and became a weighty liability in the rising flood plain. All of Sisera's troops were destroyed by the advancing Israelites who had the high ground and the inspiration of Deborah the prophetess on their side. Sisera fled his mired chariot from the rear of the company and ran for his life. Sisera found his way northward, probably on his way to Hazor where Jabin would provide him safe haven. However, after forty miles of running and hiking, the exhausted Sisera took refuge in the camp of Heber and looked to Heber's wife, Jael for hospitality and refuge. He did not count on a woman rising up in the anointing of Deborah.

Jael knew that her husband had chosen foolishly to aid the enemy in opposition to God's people. Jael's name means, "Climber; a wild goat; chamois; gazelle; from the root meaning to profit; to ascend, to help; benefit." Jael determined to climb up on the Lord's side, benefit Deborah and profit spiritually. She gave Sisera some fresh milk, which helped him to fall asleep quickly. Then with stealth and great courage, Jael sneaked into the tent with hammer and tent peg in hand. This powerful woman rose up in courage and executed the Lord's enemy by smashing a tent peg through his temple with a hammer.

Jael was a wild woman who climbed up in courage to benefit the kingdom of God. **"The high hills are for the wild goats; the cliffs are a refuge for the rock badgers" (Psalms 104:18).** Jael represents a prophetic intercessor who ascends unto Zion and does spiritual warfare to help set people free. She puts to death the intellectual pride of man and goes by the Spirit in all things. There are many Jaels today who are married to compromising Hebers. Operating by sight, Hebers are carnal men married to on fire women who are passionate for Jesus. Due to fear and jealousy, many Hebers resist the Holy Spirit and try to control their wives' behavior. They may succeed for a season, but Jael will pray and wait for her moment to rise up. Hebers eventually repent, die or learn to keep quiet while their wives go off to the prayer meetings and do battle in the name of the Lord. Deborah prophesied that a woman would get the glory instead of Barak and it happened just as she said. Jael's action, hammering death to Sisera's head, is a prophetic picture of the warfare prophesied by Zechariah below.

The Sons of Zion Against the Sons of Greece

"As for you also, because of the blood of your covenant, I will set your prisoners free from the waterless pit. Return to the stronghold, you prisoners of hope. Even today I declare that I will restore double to you. For I have bent Judah, My bow, fitted the bow with Ephraim, and raised up your sons, O Zion, against your sons, O Greece, and made you like the sword of a mighty man."

Then the LORD will be seen over them, and His arrow will go forth like lightning. The Lord GOD will blow the trumpet, and go with whirlwinds from the south. The LORD of hosts will defend them; they shall devour and subdue with slingstones. They shall drink and roar as if with wine; they shall be filled with blood like basins, like the corners of the altar. The LORD their God will save them in that day, as the flock of His people. For they shall be like the jewels of a crown, lifted like a banner over His land— For how great is its goodness and how great its beauty! Grain shall make the young men thrive, and new wine the young women. Zechariah 9:11-17

Deborah was from the tribe of Ephraim. Zechariah declared that God bends the bow of Judah and fits it with the arrows of Ephraim. Zechariah prophesied that God would raise up the sons of Zion to come against the sons of Greece. Sons of Zion walk by the anointing and follow the prophetic flow of the Holy Spirit by putting their faith in His voice. Deborah operated by the prophetic voice of God. Her words were fitted in the bow of God and went forth. Spiritual warfare took place in the heavenlies and God released His angels to fight for Israel. Sisera was a picture of a son of Greece who operated by natural wisdom and Jael put a tent peg through that head.

Sons of Greece operate by human wisdom, self-effort

and the plans of man. When they infiltrate the minds of church leaders, a Pharisaic religion is the end result. In these last days, God will use prophetic Christians who walk by the prophetic anointing of the Holy Spirit to challenge those leaders in the Church who walk by the natural mind and resist the anointing.

"I will set your prisoners free from the waterless pit" is a reference to Joseph who was thrown into an empty well by his jealous brothers. Joseph represents the prophets who have been assaulted by jealous brothers whose minds are earthly and not spiritually tuned to the prophetic. God is going to set prophetic people free from the dry pits. Nearly all prophets go through the assault and captivity of "Greek" brethren who do not understand the anointing or the ways of the Spirit. These natural minded leaders walk by fear rather than faith. A leader with a heart in fear will manifest jealousy and will seek to control those who operate by the anointing of the Spirit.

The bow of Judah represents believers who get caught up in extended praise and worship that follows the anointing of the Holy Spirit. As they ascend to the heights as Deborah did, the word of the Lord is released like an arrow. When Jacob blessed Manasseh and Ephraim, the younger, he was led by the Spirit to cross his hands and bestow the greater blessing on Ephraim (see Genesis 48). This action placed Ephraim in the birthright position to inherit a double portion of the blessings of Joseph (see Genesis 49:22-26).

The arrow of Ephraim represents a double portion prophetic anointing of the last days being released from a life filled with prophetic intercession. Ephraim represents prophetic people who live by the Holy Spirit in all ways, at all times. Their words are the lightning releases of God that have revelation, authority, anointing and the power of God behind them. Deborah is a powerful illustration of this truth. She was a prophetic warrior prototype for the last days

Church. There will come a shift when God will exalt the truly anointed prophetic Deborah Church and the religious church will fade from control over the people. Many people will run from the religious traditional churches to where God's manifested presence is experienced and His voice is heard.

During extended praise and worship at our church, God often gives a prophetic intercession or action to one of the body members. The Spirit once came on me during worship for a powerful intercession for China. While nearly everyone else was standing and singing, the travail of the Spirit came upon me to release a warfare intercession for the believers in China to be loosed from captivity. I fell to my knees and prayed with great unction and fervency.

Later, I asked the Lord why the intercession came in the midst of worship. He told me that the worship created a cloud cover so that the guided arrow of prophetic intercession would come upon the enemy suddenly and he would not know who it came from. I was being protected by the cloud of God's presence created by worship, the bow of Judah, as the arrow of Ephraim was released.

God intends to release many powerful prophetic prayers and actions to tear down and assault the religious leadership of man imposed upon His Church. Many have rejected the headship of Jesus by His Spirit and have established themselves as the head of the church. The sons of Zion are going to prevail because they establish the Holy Spirit as the head of the church by His anointing.

Greeks Seek After Natural Wisdom

For Jews request a sign, and Greeks seek after wisdom; but we preach Christ crucified, to the Jews a stumbling block and to the Greeks foolishness, but to those who are called, both Jews and Greeks, Christ the power of God and the wisdom of God. Because the foolishness

of God is wiser than men, and the weakness of God is stronger than men. I Corinthians 1:22-25

Greeks seek after a natural human wisdom that James tells us is earthly, sensual and demonic (James 3:15). In most American churches, there are some "Greeks" who operate by the natural mind rather than by the revelation of the Spirit of God. Doctrines of demons have been formed by "Greeks" to discount the ministries of the Holy Spirit. Just as the Jews of Jesus' day discounted Jesus' testimony of the Father, the Greeks of our day discount the testimony of the Holy Spirit manifested through His body.

The Greek nation was formed by Javan, a descendent of Noah. The name Javan means "Supple; clay. He that deceives. A defrauder; the effervescing one; mired." The spirit of Greece seeks to mold the mind like clay and deceive the mind by building strongholds of counterfeit wisdom. The Greek mind is constantly operating or effervescing trying to figure things out. The Greek mind is mired in clay, stuck in the mud like Sisera's chariots and finds it difficult to operate by the Spirit and believe the promises of God. The Greek primarily walks by sight and not by faith.

The Spirit of Greece Enslaves the Mind

Also the people of Judah and the people of Jerusalem you have sold to the Greeks, that you may remove them far from their borders. Joel 3:6

Javan, Tubal, and Meshech were your traders. They bartered human lives and vessels of bronze for your merchandise. Ezekiel 27:13

There is a battle for the mind of believers, and the spirit of Greece will take unrepentant, soulish "Christians" captive into a religion of self-righteous works rather than a relationship with the Holy Spirit. Many believers perish because of a lack of revelation knowledge. Greeks operate by systems of thought that keep believers out of truly entering into the kingdom of God.

"Woe to you lawyers! For you have taken away the key of knowledge. You did not enter in yourselves, and those who were entering in you hindered." And as He said these things to them, the scribes and the Pharisees began to assail Him vehemently, and to cross-examine Him about many things, lying in wait for Him, and seeking to catch Him in something He might say, that they might accuse Him. Luke 11:52-54

Jesus assailed the lawyers who took away the key of knowledge. The key of knowledge is granted to those who enter into the presence of God through faith and receive revelation by the Holy Spirit. The Person of the Holy Spirit is seen as the wisdom and knowledge of God in Proverbs 8 and 9 and is called "She." All true knowledge comes by relationship to the Father through the blood of His Son and by the Holy Spirit.

But woe to you, scribes and Pharisees, hypocrites! For you shut up the kingdom of heaven against men; for you neither go in yourselves, nor do you allow those who are entering to go in. Matthew 23:13

The teaching of scribes and Pharisees that keeps people out of the kingdom of heaven did not end in the first century. Religious spirits have influenced many New Testament theologians to make up a religion of man, based on what they think the Bible means. They become blind guides leading their blind followers into a pit. We can only enter into the kingdom of heaven by a living relationship with Jesus Christ expressed in submitting daily to the leading of the Holy Spirit.

In the days of the life of Jesus, a Jew could not reject Jesus and still have a relationship with the Father. To reject

Jesus was to reject the Father because Jesus and the Father are one. Today, those who reject the ministry of the Holy Spirit do not have a relationship to the Father no matter how religious they may seem. To reject the Holy Spirit now is to reject the Father and His Son. Rejecting the Holy Spirit causes us to be "lawless" or ungoverned by the leadership of God. Many who think they are serving Jesus are lawless and will not enter into heaven (see Matthew 7:21).

Overcoming the Prince of Greece

Then he said, "Do you know why I have come to you? And now I must return to fight with the prince of Persia; and when I have gone forth, indeed <u>the prince of Greece will come</u>." Daniel 10:20 (underlining mine)

Daniel prayed and fasted three weeks to receive break-through revelation (see Daniel 9 and 10). During the intense prayers of Daniel, we learn that there was a warfare in the heavenly realms where the messenger angel Gabriel could not break through the prince of Persia and his comrades. Finally, the great warring archangel Michael was dispatched to clear the way so that Daniel could receive throne room revelation.

The angel warned Daniel that after he returned to heaven, the prince of Greece would come. This established a spiritual pattern that has been repeated throughout history. Earnest seekers of truth pray and fast to get breakthrough revelation from the Father. The warfare is intense and we occasionally must fast and pray longer than 21 days. After the revelation comes, the enemy changes tactics and sends in the prince of Greece to taint the revelation or move of the Spirit with human wisdom, human interpretation and human application.

Most genuine movements of the Holy Spirit in the last three hundred years started pure only to be taken over gradually by the prince of Greece. This prince will influence leaders to try and control and manage the movement according to their own wisdom. Before long, the presence of the Lord has left, but the form of godliness remains as a tradition to a time when the Spirit once moved. Some traditions still sing the same hymns that were once anointed several hundred years ago. The cloud moved on but they stayed put. The lawyers came in empowered by the prince of Greece and took over.

Although the Holy Spirit is all-powerful, He is easily grieved and will leave when His welcome is worn out. Sons of Zion have to continuously hunger and thirst after the presence of the Holy Spirit and abandon themselves to the prophetic voice. Spirit-filled believers must make the Holy Spirit feel welcome and allow Him to rule in their midst.

Certain Greeks Seek Jesus

Now there were certain Greeks among those who came up to worship at the feast. Then they came to Philip, who was from Bethsaida of Galilee, and asked him, saying, "Sir, we wish to see Jesus." Philip came and told Andrew, and in turn Andrew and Philip told Jesus. But Jesus answered them, saying, "The hour has come that the Son of Man should be glorified. Most assuredly, I say to you, unless a grain of wheat falls into the ground and dies, it remains alone; but if it dies, it produces much grain. He who loves his life will lose it, and he who hates his life in this world will keep it for eternal life. If anyone serves Me, let him follow Me; and where I am, there My servant will be also. If anyone serves Me, him My Father will honor. John 12:20-26

Sincere Greeks came to the Passover feast in Jerusalem and heard about Jesus. They approached Philip and requested an audience with the Lord. Jesus did not allow an interview with these Greek believers. They did not get to see Jesus. Why didn't these earnest Greeks obtain an interview with Jesus?

Jesus listened carefully to the request to meet with the Greeks, but He did not allow them to see Him. Jesus' action was prophetic. The Greek mind cannot see the things of the Spirit. The Greek mind will not be allowed to see Jesus. The Lord Jesus knew that Greeks were seeking after human wisdom and with them in mind, He responded by teaching us how to come out from under the spirit of Greece.

"The hour has come that the Son of Man should be glorified." We must seek to glorify the Son of Man in everything we say and do. Jesus was glorified in the cross event as He demonstrated His infinite love and grace for lost sinners. Jesus called us to take up our cross and follow Him (Luke 9:23). Embracing the cross daily is foolishness to proud Greeks who want to live by the natural mind.

Jesus used the title "Son of Man" here, which was also used 80 times to describe Ezekiel, the most mystical of all the prophets. Ezekiel was completely abandoned to the Spirit and lived a very strange life according to our standards. Deborah lived her life abandoned to the Spirit and led the nation into battle against the intellectual pride of Jabin and Sisera. Jesus lived by the Holy Spirit at all times, and we must seek to live like Him. Jesus only spoke what was revealed to him by the Father (John 12:49).

"Most assuredly, I say to you, unless a grain of wheat falls into the ground and dies, it remains alone; but if it dies, it produces much grain." The grain of wheat is a parable or illustration that the head, natural wisdom, must die, must come down in humility and be buried in the ground. We should ask Jael to pass that tent peg and put to death our carnal wisdom. The Greeks operated and looked for natural wisdom. Therefore, the cross was foolishness to them. They were also very earthly and practical and not given at all to living by the Spirit. Jesus illustrated that as long as we live by natural wisdom, like the grain of wheat still on top of the stalk, we do not have true life and cannot reproduce any life or fruit.

"He who loves his life will lose it, and he who hates his life in this world will keep it for eternal life." Jesus followed up the grain illustration with clear teaching that the individual that loves his life, natural wisdom, opinions and carnal thoughts, would lose it. Loving one's life means to live by the strength of the natural man independent of the Holy Spirit. Those who lose their life recognize that there is no goodness in natural wisdom or the self-life. They choose to hate the self-life because it is full of evil, like Satan who is full of self-worship. The one who hates eating from the tree of knowledge of good and evil, will eat from the tree of life, the revelation knowledge from Jesus. Those who operate by the tree of life find eternal life in Christ.

"If anyone serves Me, let him follow Me; and where I am, there My servant will be also. If anyone serves Me, him My Father will honor." The final principle in overcoming the Prince of Greece is to serve and follow Jesus. The self-life is completely denied and there is no self-focus. The only focus is a life of service, obedience and following the will of Jesus who only did the will of the Father and said what was told to Him by the Father. The servant of Jesus will seek out the presence of the Lord (the anointing) and will become one with the anointing. The Father will honor the servant who lives by the anointing.

Deborah's prophetic ministry and Jael's powerful action against Sisera's brain are a powerful picture of how God will come against the natural Greek mindsets. He will exalt those who abandon their own minds to allow the mind of the Spirit to lead them in all things.

Iron Chariots Versus Chariots of Fire

Sisera had 900 iron chariots at his disposal. These represent the vehicles of man's power and are often seen in man's strategies, programs and systems of operations. Iron chariots are symbols of the weapons of demonic warfare. Some ministries are like machines that develop powerful strategies and systems to build a bigger church through programmed religion. The strength of their facilities and programs sometimes overwhelm and conquer God's people. Chariots also speaks of high authority in the spiritual realm. Iron speaks of earthly, sensual and demonic wisdom and is hardened to the ways of the Spirit (James 3:15).

The chariots of God are twenty thousand, even thousands of thousands; the Lord is among them as in Sinai, in the Holy Place. Psalm 68:17

For behold, the LORD will come with fire and with His chariots, like a whirlwind, to render His anger with fury, and His rebuke with flames of fire. For by fire and by His sword the LORD will judge all flesh; and the slain of the LORD shall be many. Isaiah 66:15,16

God's angelic forces are much more powerful than those of the enemy. They are empowered in response to our prophetic intercession. This type of prayer only occurs through the Deborahs who learn to walk by the Spirit and abandon themselves to the Holy Spirit's leadership. As we learn to pray and move in the prophetic of Ephraim, the Lord will release His angels to go before us and devastate the enemy's opposition.

"Is not My word like a fire?" says the LORD, "And like a hammer that breaks the rock in pieces?" Jeremiah 23:29

You are My battle-ax and weapons of war: for with you I will break the nation in pieces; with you I will destroy kingdoms; with you I will break in pieces the

horse and its rider; with you I will break in pieces the chariot and its rider. Jeremiah 51:20,21

God's anointed prophetic word is like a fire, a hammer and a battle-ax. Jeremiah walked in that level of the prophetic and so did Deborah. We have not known this level of the prophetic word because we have been filled with the mixture of this world. God is training Nazarite prophets in the hiding places of the earth. They will not move with flattery or divination. They will not prophesy for profit or fear man. God will rise up a holy army of warrior prophets like Deborah whose word has the anointing of fire on it. God will use them as His battle-ax and weapons of war. The words of anointed last-day prophets will bring down the kingdoms of man.

God's anointed voice is powerful to shake everything that can be shaken on the earth. When the Deborah Church arises in true prophetic purity, she will shake the nations with the voice of the Lord. Her decrees will break in pieces the chariots of the enemy. Her words will be the hammer of Jael that will destroy the strongholds of man built in the minds of many captives. God is going to loose such incredible anointing, power and authority to a few holy women that it will astound men in Church leadership today. Those who are wise will walk like Barak and get into agreement with them.

The fire of God is being released today to purge the daughters of Zion of filth so they can become a pure and holy dwelling place for the power of the Holy Spirit to be loosed (see Isaiah 4). We are to become the chariots of God's holy fire and minister under the zeal and passion of the Spirit of Elijah and John the Baptist. Intercessors must call upon the name of the Lord for His anointing to prepare the way and to bring in the latter rain for the coming of the Lord is at hand!

CHAPTER 9

DEBORAH'S VICTORY SONG

"Then Deborah and Barak the son of Abinoam sang on that day" (Judges 5:1a). The prophetic song anointing came upon Deborah and Barak to celebrate one of the greatest military victories of the Canaan conquest. The song exalted God for His mighty power in delivering Israel from an oppressive enemy. The song tells us that Sisera's chariots were overwhelmed by the miraculous flash flood in the Kishon River valley. Moses sang a similar song of triumph over the chariots of Pharaoh when the water crushed them (Exodus 15). God crushes the chariots of the enemy with the outpoured water of His Spirit!

The Bride of Christ will sing along with her beloved Bridegroom when the victory of God is complete on Earth. The coming flood of the Holy Spirit will end Satan's rebellion at last. All those in the ark of Christ will be preserved as Noah's family was in the flood. Those who fail to enter the ark of Christ will be swept away by the flood of judgment. We will sing great songs of deliverance in days ahead. Perhaps we will sing the Song of Solomon and recount our love affair with Jesus. We will sing new songs and worship for all eternity in the triumph of our God who delivers us out of all our troubles.

When Leaders Lead

Then Deborah and Barak the son of Abinoam sang on that day, saying: "When leaders lead in Israel, when the people willingly offer themselves, bless the LORD! Hear, O kings! Give ear, O princes! I, even I, will sing to the LORD; I will sing praise to the LORD God of Israel." Judges 5:1-3

When anointed leaders truly lead by the Spirit of God and tap into His prophetic power, many people will follow in the freedom of the Spirit. The people willingly offer themselves as volunteers in the day of God's power (Psalm 110:3). Under the anointing of the Holy Spirit, when leaders and people work in perfect unity by the Spirit, it is time to bless the Lord and sing!

The phrase **"when leaders lead"** is the translation of the two similar Hebrew words, "para'" and "par'ah." Para' means "to loosen; by implication, to expose, dismiss; figuratively, absolve, begin" and is translated in the KJV "avenge, avoid, bare, go back, let, (make) naked, set at nought, perish, refuse, uncover." The NKJV, NIV and ASV translate the phrase, "when leaders (princes) lead." Par'ah means "leadership (plural concretely, leaders)" and is translated in the KJV as "avenging, revenge." Par'ah is the feminine form of the root word "pera." Pera means "the hair (as disheveled)" and is translated "locks." Some scholars have translated it "the hair let down," the implication being that the leaders loosen their hair. This means that they become completely vulnerable and free to flow in the Spirit.

"The hair let down" may also be a picture of leaders becoming Nazarites who are totally separated unto God and walking holy before Him in His power. When the Spirit of the Lord has complete possession of a person, there is liberty for God to move through them in power. Since parah is a feminine form of pera, it points to women leaders who let their hair down and are loosed into leadership. This refers to Deborah's leadership and is a prophetic vision of women and the bride of the last days. Deborah was loosed to lead by the Spirit and the people willingly followed her leadership. When anointed women completely sanctify themselves unto God like Nazarites and are loosed into their place of leadership, kings and princes will take notice. The Deborah Church will freely follow those anointed leaders and will rise up in high praise by His Spirit.

Let the high praises of God be in their mouth, and a two-edged sword in their hand, to execute vengeance on the nations, and punishments on the peoples; to bind their kings with chains, and their nobles with fetters of iron; to execute on them the written judgment—this honor have all His saints. Praise the LORD! Psalms 149:6-9

God is raising up many women worship leaders under the prophetic song anointing to lead the people in high praise. The Lord releases a powerful warfare through anointed prophetic praise that does incredible battle in the heavenlies. Deborah was a prophetic worshipper who led her people in high praise. She exhorted the kings and princes to hear her testimony of praise and join with her in blessing the Lord and singing praise to the Lord God of Israel. Deborah's song became a powerful prophetic declaration and was sung by great and small for many years as a reminder of God's powerful deliverance.

The Clouds Pour Down Rain

LORD, when You went out from Seir, when You marched from the field of Edom, the earth trembled and

the heavens poured, the clouds also poured water; the mountains gushed before the LORD, this Sinai, before the LORD God of Israel. In the days of Shamgar, son of Anath, in the days of Jael, the highways were deserted, and the travelers walked along the byways. Village life ceased, it ceased in Israel, until I, Deborah, arose, arose a mother in Israel. They chose new gods; then there was war in the gates; not a shield or spear was seen among forty thousand in Israel. My heart is with the rulers of Israel who offered themselves willingly with the people. Bless the LORD! Speak, you who ride on white donkeys, who sit in judges' attire, and who walk along the road. Far from the noise of the archers, among the watering places, there they shall recount the righteous acts of the LORD, the righteous acts for His villagers in Israel; then the people of the LORD shall go down to the gates. Judges 5:4-11**

As God had visited Israel at Mount Sinai in a dark, fiery cloud flashing with lightning, thundering and smoke, so the God of Israel heard Deborah's impassioned intercession and came in a dark cloud and poured out His wrath upon His enemies. The earth trembled from the thunderous blasts and the cloudburst poured rain down from above causing a flash flood that washed God's enemies away. This was a major breakthrough by one woman's prayer that should inspire women of all ages to press in and pray down God's deliverance.

Our God is a wrathful God to be feared. When His people broke His covenant, the curses of Deuteronomy 28 came against them in the form of Jabin's oppression for twenty years. When Israel repented and came back into the covenant that God made on Sinai, their awesome God came down in the dark cloud to deliver them from the enemy.

The root cause of all oppression of believers is stated succinctly by Deborah, **"They chose new gods; then there was

war in the gates." When believers succumb to idolatry and selfish interests, there is division within churches. The elders ruled in the gates of the city and administered justice by God's Law. When the elders chose other gods, they could no longer heal the sick or dispense the word of the Lord. In this condition, the gates of hell began to prevail over the Church. These new gods were the Canaanite Baals who promised fertility and prosperity. The Israelites were deceived and came into agreement believing Baal opened wombs and poured out rain. God dramatically demonstrated in this battle that He is the God of rain and blessing, not Baal.

Village life ceased because the people were not safe from the assaults of Jabin's raiding armies. They had to move to larger walled cities. Jabin controlled the main highways and all normal commerce was shut down. People had to travel on the byways instead of the highways. They operated in fear and could not even properly farm the land. Livestock were not safe from raiding bands. The spirit of poverty came over the people who were locked up in abusive tyranny. There are hundreds of millions of women and men locked up in poverty in the world. We need to press in to God and get the anointing to deliver them!

"Not a shield or spear was seen among forty thousand in Israel." The enemy disarmed the children of God so they could not defend their land. Many churches today don't understand or use the weapons of spiritual warfare. The enemy has disarmed many churches by teaching false doctrines related to spiritual warfare. Some churches ignore spiritual warfare while others strongly oppose it. A demonized person can't get set free in most churches because the church is deceived or ignorant about the weapons of warfare and the invasion of the demonic in our churches. A person dying of cancer has little hope of being healed by the elders of most American churches because we have chosen other gods like entertainment, comfort, eating and drinking.

Zebulun and Naphtali experienced the oppression of Jabin the most since their land was near Hazor. Zebulun and Naphtali represent the apostolic evangelists who go out to win the lost to the Lord. The oppression of Jabin kept these tribes poor before Deborah arose. Jabin schemes to keep us in poverty without the weapons to fight or the finances to go unto the harvest. Prophetic intercession is a powerful weapon that helps us overcome Jabin's oppression. Prophetic intercession comes as the Holy Spirit tells us what to pray and gives us the unction to pray with fervency and faith. He will teach us how to pray and enable us to pray in the weapons and the finances. The Spirit will teach us how to wield the weapon of anointed prophetic declaration, which is also extremely powerful to overcome our enemies. Deborah flowed in both prophetic intercession and prophetic declaration.

"The clouds poured down rain" is a prophetic picture of the latter day rain that God will send. His outpouring will be a blessing to God's people who are positioned to flow in His Spirit and it will be a judgment to those Siseras who oppress God's people and try to prevent them from walking in their destiny. We are going to see a great outpouring of the Spirit as women arise into ministry.

Awake, Awake Deborah

Awake, awake, Deborah! Awake, awake, sing a song! Arise, Barak, and lead your captives away, O son of Abinoam! Judges 5:12

By the Spirit of God, Deborah cried unto the women of today's Church to wake up and take their place. The exhortation is greatly magnified by the fourfold exclamation, **"Awake, awake,...awake, awake!"** Women need to wake up and walk in their divine destiny. Deborah's anointed prayer resonates in the heavenlies above women. Incline your ear, hear God's voice and arise mighty women!

"Therefore He says: 'Awake, you who sleep, arise from the dead, and Christ will give you light'" (**Ephesians 5:14**). Paul confirmed Deborah's cry that the Church needs to wake up out of sleep. Part of the sleep that comes over the Church is a spirit of delusion or enchantment that counterfeits as a false peace and safety. This spirit tries to keep you from praying through by releasing a false peace that everything is going to be okay when the Lord is not saying that.

But concerning the times and the seasons, brethren, you have no need that I should write to you. For you yourselves know perfectly that the day of the Lord so comes as a thief in the night. For when they say, "<u>Peace and safety</u>!" then sudden destruction comes upon them, as labor pains upon a pregnant woman. And they shall not escape. But you, brethren, are not in darkness, so that this Day should overtake you as a thief. You are all sons of light and sons of the day. We are not of the night nor of darkness. Therefore let us not sleep, as others do, but let us watch and be sober. I Thessalonians 5:1-6 (underlining mine)

We are called by God to watch in prayer and not fall into the sleep that says you can relax and enjoy life in comfort and selfish indulgence because everything will be just fine and dandy. The message of "peace and safety" comes from the spirit of antichrist and cloaks itself as an angel of light. This lie is from hell and puts many to sleep.

The coming of the lawless one is according to the working of Satan, with all power, signs, and lying wonders, and with all unrighteous deception among those who perish, because they did not receive the love of the truth, that they might be saved. And for this reason God will send them strong delusion, that they should believe the lie, that they all may be condemned who did not believe the truth but had pleasure in unrighteousness. II

Thessalonians 2:9-12

We must love the truth of God with all our hearts devoting ourselves to prayer and the Spirit-led study of the word of God. We have to press in with the fire of God to intercede for the sure word of the Lord. Rather than relax and sleep, we need to rise up and pray, pray, pray! The enemy releases waves of fatigue, discouragement, futility, hopelessness and confusion to put women and men to sleep.

The sleep I see over women in the Spirit is rooted in four major areas. First of all, most prophetic women have not been completely healed of woundedness and rejection. Woundedness can lead to bitterness, a victim spirit and will keep you out of your Promised Land. Woundedness keeps you self-focused and under the spirit of poverty feeling sorry for yourself. That is a victim spirit. Women have basically told me that they don't run after God because they don't want to leave their husband who is walking with a limp. That is an enchantment, delusion and a lie. Staying at the same place spiritually with your carnal spouse is not going to help him grow, and it will pull you down into further bondage. Awake Deborah and come out of woundedness and run after your God!

There are many books, tapes, videos and conferences on healing the wounded heart. I know that many women have been abused and traumatized by various men. It may be a lengthy road, but God's love is enough to heal the wounded heart. Deborahs need to get healed and wake up to the call to nations. The wounded world is waiting for you to be healed and rise up. Women who become whole in the Lord will do mighty exploits for their God. Wounded women keep going around God's mountain until they get healed and are able to ascend Zion. Please get healed quickly. We need you at the front lines!

Secondly, Deborahs can temporarily get trapped in the fear of man and the bondage of man's controlling ways. This includes doctrines of demons that say that women can't, women shouldn't, women aren't supposed to lead, teach in church, pastor, be apostles, prophesy and sing their God given song. The fear of man is a snare! Run after God with reckless abandonment and fear God. Deborahs need to get out of bondage to pleasing people manifested by wanting affirmation, acceptance, popularity, appreciation and vindication from God. Deborahs need to go to the mountains of Ephraim and sit under a palm tree and pray in the Spirit. The fear of the Lord is the beginning of wisdom. Those who fear God and seek to please Him alone in all things will be overcomers.

Thirdly, women ministers can get mired in unbelief that comes by operating by sight and natural reason. Women have to go for the prophetic with all their hearts and live by the prophetic voice of God (I Corinthians 14:1). You must be extremely zealous for the prophetic anointing so that you can hear and move by the wind of God's spirit. All true faith comes by hearing the voice of God and acting on it (Romans 10:17).

Finally, women can get caught up in loving this world and loving money just as much as men do. There is a strong natural need for women to feel secure in a lovely home with adequate finances. Much devotion can be given to acquiring creature comforts and financial security. There is no such thing as financial security and creature comforts can easily be an enchantment of the enemy. The last thing any woman of God should do is give in to that entertainment spirit that so often binds up lukewarm men in the Church who spend hours watching television or pursuing some self-centered hobby. The woman of God must burn with holy fire as a prayer warrior. She must rise up and be holy no matter what her spouse does.

The love of the world is pervasive. It is the spirit of antichrist. The love of money and the desire to be rich are the root of all kinds of evil. The Lord wants to bless us abundantly with a nice home and extraordinary resources, but the pathway to His blessings is to hear His voice and obey Him. This requires that we diligently press in through extended prayer to find His voice with a heart inclined to hear and obey. God is looking for holy Nazarite women to rise up in the spirit and power of Elijah. He wants women to break off the yokes of carnal men and take the kingdom of God with violent action. It will require fasting and prayer!

There is no magic wand to heal believers from woundedness, fear of man, unbelief and love for this world. But there is infinite power in the throne room of God to heal, deliver and impart all that you need to walk in His glory. Stop making excuses, press in and break through. Take hold of the horns of the altar and don't let go until God blesses you. Awake, awake O Deborah and sing!

The Survivors Came Down to Help

Then the survivors came down, the people against the nobles; the LORD came down for me against the mighty. From Ephraim were those whose roots were in Amalek. After you, Benjamin, with your peoples, from Machir rulers came down, and from Zebulun those who bear the recruiter's staff. And the princes of Issachar were with Deborah; as Issachar, so was Barak sent into the valley under his command; among the divisions of Reuben there were great resolves of heart. Why did you sit among the sheepfolds, to hear the pipings for the flocks? The divisions of Reuben have great searchings of heart. Gilead stayed beyond the Jordan, and why did Dan remain on ships? Asher continued at the seashore, and stayed by his inlets. Zebulun is a people who jeopardized their lives to the point of death, Naphtali also, on the heights of the battlefield. Judges 5:13-18

Many women have become survivors through perseverance and many trials. They have held onto God through
extremely difficult family struggles. Other women, sad to
say, have given up and have fallen into lukewarm carnality.
The survivors become the overcomers against the demonic
powers that try to keep them in bondage.

**"From Ephraim were those whose roots were in
Amalek."** The Amalekites were the first people to oppose
Israel after they were delivered from Egypt. Moses sent
Joshua with an army to fight Amalek. Moses, Aaron and Hur
prayed on a mountain overlooking the battlefield (Exodus
17:8-16). When Moses lifted his hands in intercession, God's
people advanced against Amalek. When Moses tired and
rested from intercession, Amalek prevailed.

**Remember what Amalek did to you on the way as
you were coming out of Egypt, how he met you on the
way and attacked your rear ranks, all the stragglers at
your rear, when you were tired and weary; and he did
not fear God. Deuteronomy 25:17,18**

Amalek represents a powerful demonic spirit that
attacks God's people in their most vulnerable area. This is a
cowardly spirit that goes after the weakest members in the
body of Christ. Amalek means, "A people that lick up or
exhaust; people of lapping; a strangler of the people; war-
like; a dweller in the vale." Amalek is a predatory spirit that
seeks to exhaust your energy, vision, faith and hope. He
especially seeks to assault weak women and children.
Amalek was the descendent of Esau's first-born son Eliphaz
meaning, "My god is fine gold." Amalek's motivation is the
love of money. The only way to overcome Amalek is
through sustained intercession. In the warfare against
Amalek, Moses learned that God is "Jehovah-Nissi," The
Lord our Banner. For twenty years, Amalek took advantage
of the weakness of Israel and had made raiding assaults into
the mountains of Ephraim. This enemy marched to its doom

in the Kishon River valley.

Ephraimites are prophetic intercessors who exalt Jehovah-Nissi. The tribe of Ephraim had engaged Amalek in the natural. Ephraimite watchmen probably saw the division of troops marching to war up north and followed them. Deborah commended the warriors of Ephraim for joining the battle. God is looking for watchwomen to watch and pray. He will commend you for your warfare.

Soldiers from Benjamin and Machir, half of the tribe of Manasseh, also joined the war and are commended for their involvement. Benjamin means "Son of the right hand" and was the twelfth born and last son of Jacob. Benjamin represents the last-day apostles and was prototyped in the life of the apostle Paul who was of the tribe of Benjamin. The Benjamites were great warriors and provided tremendous aid in the battle against Sisera.

The tribe of Reuben could not decide whether to join the battle or not and stayed neutral. They had great searchings of heart but ultimately did nothing. Perhaps they had the paralysis of analysis. Many Christians stay out of the battles of the Lord because they are not sure what to do. The Lord rebuked Reuben as well as Gilead, Dan and Asher for not coming to the aid of Deborah and Barak. God could easily win the fight without them, but He calls for His people to fight in unity. God is not looking for ivory tower theologians or theoretical Christians. He is looking for warriors who will volunteer to fight in the day of God's power. This is the day of God's power and the fields are white unto harvest. Every believer should be involved in missions at some level.

Our church supports evangelism and missionary pastors overseas. We send mission teams out several times a year to do ministry. We believe that everyone who is able should go on a mission trip in season and minister in the power of the Spirit. Mission trips are life changing experiences but also can include intense warfare and personal discomfort. We pay for our own trips and give freely expecting nothing in return because we usually minister to the poor. God wants Deborahs to rise up and go out to war in missions. Most Christians can go on a trip at least once every few years. Others can stay home and pray for them. The battles are out there! God's people need help evangelizing their nation and praying back the Amalekites and fighting the devils of that area.

We must all appear before the Judgment Seat of Christ, and each one will answer for what he or she has done in the body whether good or evil (II Corinthians 5:10). Those who have joined in the battles of the Lord will be affirmed, commended and rewarded. Those who stayed with their own selfish interests will be judged by the Lord. They may go to heaven, but they will lose certain rewards that could have been theirs.

They Fought From the Heavens

The kings came and fought, then the kings of Canaan fought in Taanach, by the waters of Megiddo; they took no spoils of silver. They fought from the heavens; the stars from their courses fought against Sisera. The torrent of Kishon swept them away, that ancient torrent, the torrent of Kishon. O my soul, march on in strength! Then the horses' hooves pounded, the galloping, galloping of his steeds. "Curse Meroz," said the angel of the LORD, "Curse its inhabitants bitterly, because they did not come to the help of the LORD, to the help of the LORD against the mighty." Judges 5:19-23

Jabin had alliance with many regional kings and they joined with him in the battle to destroy Israel. These kings represent principalities and powers that seek to destroy God's people today. God's angelic beings fought from the heavens against them and brought a powerful rainstorm complete with bolts of lightning, frightening thunder, dark clouds, hail stones and intense rain. The rain caused the tributaries that fed the Kishon to merge into an incredible flash flood that crushed the power of Sisera's horses and chariots.

Water and rain represents the outpouring of the Holy Spirit against whom no enemy can stand. As the remnants of Sisera's army fled, they went through an ancient town called Meroz, which was cursed because it refused to stand with God's people. The angel of the Lord will curse many who do not aid Christians in their day of calamity. Meroz disappeared from history and withered and died like the fig tree Christ cursed.

There were many support personnel for the army of Sisera who were unarmed servants and included many women and children. Barak, the son of Abinoam overcame them and did not kill them. He took them into captivity and led them as his captives. This is a picture of Christ who conquered hell and led captives away (see Psalm 68:18; Ephesians 4:8). King David sang an anointed warfare psalm in honor of God's mighty works that included scenes from the great battle of Deborah and Barak.

Then the earth shook and trembled; the foundations of the hills also quaked and were shaken, because He was angry. Smoke went up from His nostrils, and devouring fire from His mouth; coals were kindled by it. He bowed the heavens also, and came down with darkness under His feet. And He rode upon a cherub, and flew; He flew upon the wings of the wind. He made darkness His secret place; His canopy around Him was dark waters and thick clouds of the skies. From the brightness before Him, His thick clouds passed with hailstones and coals of fire. The LORD also thundered from heaven, and the Most High uttered His voice, hailstones and coals of fire. He sent out His arrows and scattered the foe, lightnings in abundance, and He vanquished them. Psalm 18:7-14

Blessed is Courageous Jael

Most blessed among women is Jael, the wife of Heber the Kenite; blessed is she among women in tents. He asked for water, she gave milk; she brought out cream in a lordly bowl. She stretched her hand to the tent peg, her right hand to the workmen's hammer; she pounded Sisera, she pierced his head, she split and struck through his temple. At her feet he sank, he fell, he lay still; at her feet he sank, he fell; where he sank, there he fell dead. Judges 5:24-27

Jael is honored through all history for her valor and courage in putting Sisera to death. Even though her husband was a compromising carnal man, Jael undoubtedly watched and prayed for her opportunity to rise up in the anointing of God. She was a domestic woman who served dutifully for many years. Long hours, little thanks and great responsibilities were her lot in life. She ran the household and ran for Heber. She was a resourceful woman to whom the Lord chose to give honor. Many women, who are serving in domestic roles, are waiting for the Lord's release and for their divine moment. Jael got her moment and she did not fail.

This undercover wild woman played along with Sisera for a brief time. She played the ruse to the fullest by giving him cream in her finest china. Jael was an expert in reading the body language of powerful men. She had probably seen Sisera before in his proud demeanor laughing and talking politics with Heber. She had served Sisera the best foods and drinks they could offer as Heber looked for business opportunities with Jabin. On this day, Jael knew that Sisera was a defeated general. Perhaps Sisera had treated her with contempt on other occasions. No matter, Jael decided to take the Lord's side and finish what Deborah and Barak had begun. She pierced Sisera's head with a tent peg. Perhaps the first

171

blow did not do him in and he sat up in astonishment. Jael completed her mission as he fell at her feet.

The Siseras of this world have loved money and carnal pleasure. They have gone out as businessmen to conquer and take spoils. The love of money has pierced them with many sorrows and their doom is as certain as Sisera (I Timothy 6:9,10).

The Women of Sisera

The mother of Sisera looked through the window, and cried out through the lattice, "Why is his chariot so long in coming? Why tarries the clatter of his chariots?" Her wisest ladies answered her, yes, she answered herself, "Are they not finding and dividing the spoil: to every man a girl or two; for Sisera, plunder of dyed garments, plunder of garments embroidered and dyed, two pieces of dyed embroidery for the neck of the looter?" Thus let all Your enemies perish, O LORD! Judges 5:28-31a

In contrast to the righteous Deborah and Jael are the women of Sisera who fantasized of fine clothing and the spoils of war. They longed for the riches of this world and had many servants to flatter them in their selfish indulgence. They had no concern for the pillage and plunder of the poor Hebrew children whom they despised. They felt it a just reward for Sisera and his men to each ravage a young maid or two.

Their impatience exposes their carnal hearts that longed for sensual pleasures. Having rejected the ways of the Lord, they made their belly a god and the exploitation of the needy their carnal ambition. They loved the finer things in life and despised the poor in their arrogance. The enemies of God, like Sisera, end their days with a lordly bowl of cream and go to sleep satisfied that their belly is full. They ate, drank and were merry thinking that there was no judgment. Their sleep and slumber was an enchantment of hell. Their awakening before the white throne of God is the beginning of their eternal nightmare in outer darkness.

Arise and Shine like the Sun

But let those who love Him be like the sun when it comes out in full strength. So the land had rest for forty years. Judges 5:31b

The warriors who love God and join Him in His battles shall be transformed by knowing God intimately and fighting for His causes. They shall rise up in the glory of God's light in the midst of the darkness around them. Even though the enemy sends resistance and persecution against prophetic women, they shake off the dust, take back their peace and move on to the next mission from the Lord.

Arise, shine; for your light has come! And the glory of the LORD is risen upon you. For behold, the darkness shall cover the earth, and deep darkness the people; but the LORD will arise over you, and His glory will be seen upon you. The Gentiles shall come to your light, and kings to the brightness of your rising. Isaiah 60:1-3

Deborah's song is echoed in Isaiah's exhortation for women of faith to arise in the light and glory of the Lord. Even as the darkness increases on the earth, the light of those separated unto God shall increase. The lost will come to your light and kings to the brightness of your rising. Women have a great inheritance in the Lord as sons of the most high God. As you arise into it, God will give you your divine moment so that He can honor you throughout eternity.

Deborah went into prophetic warfare in the Spirit and then brought God's power into the natural realm to deliver the troops who obeyed God's voice. Deborah's victory song celebrated the triumph and began a season of forty years of rest for the land. The Israelites forsook the Baals who promised them fertility and prosperity but gave them futility and poverty. As they returned to worshipping their Creator and obeying God's Law, the blessings of God poured out and He restored what the locusts had consumed. Village life was restored. The highways were opened. There was justice in the land. The people knew their God was mighty and worshipped Him only. The land was at rest.

CHAPTER 10

AWAKE O DEBORAH AND SING

Awake, awake, Deborah! Awake, awake, sing a song! Arise, Barak, and lead your captives away, O son of Abinoam! Judges 5:12

The heart cry of ancient Deborah is that modern Deborahs would awaken out of sleep and sing their song. The overwhelming challenges of living in the natural realm can put us to sleep to the greater reality of walking in the kingdom of God. Most Christians are asleep in awareness to spiritual dynamics and the call of God on their lives. Your song is to walk in your divine destiny and bear much fruit for the glory of God. The Lord has a specific purpose and destiny for you. We need a great awakening so we can see and run with God's vision for our lives.

Deborah's victory song is the second great victory song recorded in the Bible. The first triumphant song was given to Moses after God delivered the children of Israel from Pharaoh's mighty army of chariots. This extraordinary victory warranted a song for the ages as God completed His deliverance of His people out of Egypt.

Deborah's prophetic song celebrates God's supernatural intervention to deliver His people in the Promised Land from their wicked Canaanite oppressors. God first delivers us out of Egypt and then works to get Egypt out of us. The battles and struggles that we must overcome in order to walk in our divine destiny are designed to purge the remnants of Egypt from us.

As we violently war to take hold of our divine destiny in Christ, the Canaanite oppression resists our taking hold of all that God has blessed us with in the heavenly places in Christ Jesus. The Lord wants us to possess our inheritance, which is nothing less than God Himself, the Spirit without measure (Ezekiel 44:28; John 3:34).

When we offer ourselves unreservedly to the Lord and draw near to Him, God will draw near to us (Romans 12:1,2; James 4:8). As He possesses us, we will possess Him. When we become one with Him, He can flow His love through us in Spirit and truth with power. We must have victory over Sisera and Jabin and operate in the fullness of the Holy Spirit to conquer Canaanite devils and take possession of our destiny.

Take Your Promised Land by Violent Warfare

Blessed be the God and Father of our Lord Jesus Christ, who has blessed us with every spiritual blessing in the heavenly places in Christ. Ephesians 1:3

God has already blessed Christians with every spiritual blessing needed to overcome the world, the flesh and the devil and walk in the blessings of God. However, all of those blessings are **"in the heavenly places"** and must be brought into the natural realm. Your destiny of fruit bearing ministry that glorifies God is part of your spiritual blessing. Health, holiness, the anointing, authority, power and divine prosperity are a few of those spiritual blessings. To appropriate these blessings that have already been paid for by Christ, we must take violent action.

"And from the days of John the Baptist until now the kingdom of heaven suffers violence, and the violent take it by force" (Matthew 11:12). John the Baptist was filled with the Holy Spirit and separated himself from the world during his childhood. He grew strong in spirit and grew up in desert places. John fasted, prayed, and sought the Lord with the intense zeal of Elijah. I believe Deborah did the same. Violent warfare begins by repenting of our sins and learning to love the Lord our God with all our heart, soul, mind and strength. We must forsake the world, and run after God.

The people of God entered the Promised Land by the miraculous provision of God through a rolled back Jordan River. They took Jericho by violent action with supernatural help as the walls fell down. The campaign of possessing your personal destiny follows the same pattern. The Holy Spirit leads you and works with you to take hold of what God has promised you. This requires a holy violence seen in John the Baptist who walked in the spirit and power of Elijah.

As we search for God with all our hearts as John did, the Holy Spirit separates us from the religious establishment of our day that has the traditions of man influencing them. John sought God with everything in Him and fasted and prayed to know His God. He went into the wilderness to seek the Lord and found his God and his mission in life. There was no greater natural man ever born. His life is a pattern.

Perhaps there was no greater woman born in history than Deborah. She went into the mountains of Ephraim and sought the Lord. She was a worshipper and prayer warrior who earnestly took hold of the horns of the altar and prayed until she found her God. **"So I sought for a man among them who would make a wall, and stand in the gap before Me on behalf of the land, that I should not destroy**

it; but I found no one" (Ezekiel 22:30). The Lord couldn't find a man to stand in the gap during Israel's idolatry, but He found a woman who prayed with fervent intercession. She built a spiritual wall as she petitioned the Lord to deliver Israel from disgrace. As Deborah stood in the gap before God, the entire nation eventually recognized the anointing on her and submitted to her role as a national judge.

As we earnestly seek God, two things must occur. We must repent and believe. This was the basic message of John that prepared the way for the glory of the Lord to come. Our flesh must be crucified with Christ, and we must receive the impartation of faith in God so as to behold Him and become like Him (II Corinthians 3:18). There is a battle to seek God and press through the flesh and the demonic resistance.

Between the believer and all the blessings of God, which are ours in Christ Jesus, are demonic hosts that resist us. As we ascend unto the full measure of the stature, which belongs to Christ, the devil in our way will often have the name of our most flagrant character weakness. We cannot ascend unto a mature "man" in Christ with pride, lust, love for this world, fear of man, carnality, laziness, gluttony, love of money, outbursts of anger and all manners of flesh. The Lord will bring our flesh to His light as we ascend unto Him. He will allow us to be buffeted in our flesh by the enemy who exposes our weakness. The Spirit will enable us to crucify our flesh and walk in pure passion for Christ and obedience to His word.

Jabin and Sisera were allowed to oppress the people of God because the children of Israel decided to choose new gods, who were not gods at all but devils of hell. Demon gods' only intent is to bind up, steal, kill and destroy the child of God. Even though Christians may be saved and on their way to eternal bliss in heaven, the enemy tries to keep us pinned down and ineffective in the Promised Land of our inheritance. The Lord calls us to drive the enemy entirely out of our lives by submitting our will to the yoke of Jesus Christ and by coming into complete agreement with His life by the Spirit (Matthew 11:28-30).

Search for God with All Your Heart

Some months ago, I had a dream in which a man, whom I believe was an angel, appeared to me and said earnestly, "If you search for Him with all your heart, you will find Him!" I was very busy during a ministry conference at the time of this dream and traveled extensively for the next several months doing ministry. After three months, my schedule calmed down and the Spirit pulled me into a fast, in part, to write this book. I began searching for God with all my heart and remembered the dream one Thursday night. I knew that promise was in Jeremiah and discovered the verse in the context of Jeremiah 29.

For I know the thoughts that I think toward you, says the LORD, thoughts of peace and not of evil, to give you a future and a hope. Then you will call upon Me and go and pray to Me, and I will listen to you. And you will seek Me and find Me, when you search for Me with all your heart. I will be found by you, says the LORD, and I will bring you back from your captivity. Jeremiah 29:11-14a

When I read this passage under God's anointing, I heard the message of this word with the hearing of faith. Jeremiah was a holy prophet who called God's people to repent of their idolatries. Because they refused to repent, God warned them of an invasion from the north that would bring them into captivity. The leaders rejected Jeremiah and beat him as if he were a false prophet. Nebuchadnezzar's Babylonian army came in as prophesied and killed many of God's people and took the nobles into captivity.

The Lord told Jeremiah that their captivity was going to benefit them in the long run. The religious system had become so idolatrous and full of false prophets that God had to demonstrate His judgment so as to deliver the nation out of idolatry. Chapter 29 is Jeremiah's letter written to those in the captivity. He told them that after 70 years God would be found by them and they would be delivered from Babylon. Daniel sought God earnestly with prayer and fasting and received revelation about this word (see Daniel 9,10). God restored the nation to the Promised Land as He declared.

The principle seen in Jeremiah works in specific application for the believer who is searching for God with all her heart. We each have measures of captivities that the enemy has put on us at some point in our lives. Most of us still need emotional healing and deliverance from the fear of man at a deeper level. We all need an increase in faith in God. As we search for God with all our heart as Deborah and John did, we will find Him, and He will deliver us out of our captivity. In finding God, we find a revelation of His nature by the "hearing of faith."

The Hearing of Faith

This only I want to learn from you: did you receive the Spirit by the works of the law, or by the hearing of faith? Are you so foolish? Having begun in the Spirit, are you now being made perfect by the flesh? Have you suffered so many things in vain—if indeed it was in vain? Therefore He who supplies the Spirit to you and works miracles among you, does He do it by the works of the law, or by the hearing of faith?—just as Abraham "believed God, and it was accounted to him for righteousness." Galatians 3:2-6

Paul taught the Galatians that the supply of the Holy Spirit and the working of miracles came through the **"hearing of faith."** This kind of faith was represented by

Abraham's believing God's incredible word that he was going to have as many descendants as the stars in the sky (Genesis 15:1-6). Even though Abraham and Sarah's physical bodies were incapable of bearing seed, Abraham believed God and it was accounted to Him as righteousness. Miraculous power flowed through Abraham and Sarah's faith to enable their bodies to produce Isaac.

We cannot take the Promised Land of our inheritance, our divine destiny in God, without the hearing of faith and the miraculous power of the Holy Spirit helping us. Deborah and Barak heard the Lord and acted in faith. They would not have overcome Sisera's army without the supernatural supply of God's power seen in lightning, thunder, hailstones and rain that frightened the horses and mired the chariots in mud. Sisera's army retreated down the Kishon river valley and was overcome by a flash flood.

The principle remains the same for today. We must have God's help to conquer the enemies that keep us from our destiny. For women, there are great obstacles to overcome. Women must search for God with all their hearts and allow the Holy Spirit to bring their flesh under the cross. They must receive the impartation of faith and obey what they hear by the Spirit of the living God. Along with the hearing of faith is the prayer of faith that James taught God's people.

The Prayer of Faith

Is anyone among you sick? Let him call for the elders of the church, and let them pray over him, anointing him with oil in the name of the Lord. And the prayer of faith will save the sick, and the Lord will raise him up. And if he has committed sins, he will be forgiven. Confess your trespasses to one another, and pray for one another, that you may be healed. The effective, fervent prayer of a righteous man avails much. Elijah was a man with a

nature like ours, and he prayed earnestly that it would not rain; and it did not rain on the land for three years and six months. And he prayed again, and the heaven gave rain, and the earth produced its fruit. James 5:14-18

It is the divine destiny of the Church to walk in authority over all sickness and disease that Satan sends against her. James instructed God's people on the practice of the early Church so that they could continue to hold the ground that Jesus paid for by His stripes (I Peter 2:24). The elders were to pray in faith for the sick person and the prayer of faith would raise him up. What does the prayer of faith look like? It looks exactly like what Elijah did to bring the rain into the natural realm by God's word.

Elijah sought God earnestly and was extremely zealous to know the God of Israel. John the Baptist modeled the same level of intensity and zeal. Elijah searched for God with all His heart. The Lord told him to shut up the heavens and Elijah did. Then the Lord told him to present himself to Ahab and that rain would come (I Kings 18:1). Elijah believed God's word and obeyed.

Then Elijah said to Ahab, "Go up, eat and drink; for there is the sound of abundance of rain." So Ahab went up to eat and drink. And Elijah went up to the top of Carmel; then he bowed down on the ground, and put his face between his knees, and said to his servant, "Go up now, look toward the sea." So he went up and looked, and said, "There is nothing." And seven times he said, "Go again." Then it came to pass the seventh time, that he said, "There is a cloud, as small as a man's hand, rising out of the sea!" So he said, "Go up, say to Ahab, 'Prepare your chariot, and go down before the rain stops you.'" Now it happened in the meantime that the sky became black with clouds and wind, and there was a heavy rain. So Ahab rode away and went to Jezreel.

Then the hand of the LORD came upon Elijah; and he girded up his loins and ran ahead of Ahab to the entrance of Jezreel. 1 Kings 18:41-46

Elijah earnestly searched for God and heard in faith God's will. Then Elijah declared the will of God to Ahab as a prophetic declaration. Next Elijah had to pray in faith to bring the promised rain into the natural realm. Elijah prayed seven times symbolizing the complete measure that the Holy Spirit required. Finally the rain manifested.

This pattern demonstrates the way of the Holy Spirit that Deborah learned by the Spirit. Deborah was also extremely zealous for her God. She earnestly sought the Lord and was a prophetic intercessor. She heard God's voice on many issues and sought Him about the deliverance of Israel. Deborah called Barak and gave Him God's word to gather ten thousand troops on Mount Tabor. These soldiers had no swords or spears, but they had a word from God and a powerful intercessor with them. Do you think the violent rainstorm that came was a coincidence? No! Deborah prayed it in just as Elijah did! She knew the exact timing of the Lord and that is why Barak wanted her to go up with him. He recognized the anointing on her to intercede.

Few Christians have soundness of mind in the ways of the Spirit and the way that the spiritual realm works. God gave Elijah and Deborah high level prophetic words, but He required prevailing intercession to bring it forth from the spiritual realm into the natural realm. It is exactly the same today! God is no respecter of persons. If anyone ought to know how to bare down and birth, it should be women. Birthing prayer is needed to bring in the latter rain of God's anointing. Deborah did it for her day and you can do it for your day!

Before the rain comes, the fire comes first. Elijah prayed down fire on the altar he repaired as a demonstration that God is the Lord (I Kings 18:37ff). The people were double minded and needed to repent. The people responded in faith and helped Elijah kill the prophets of Baal. The fire of burning and judgment must come first to cleanse the daughters of Zion of their filth (see Isaiah 4). As the fire cleanses us and baptizes us, we will increase in fervency and the zeal of the Lord as Deborah, Elijah and John did. Then we can pray in the rain of the last-day outpouring and God will hear our prayers. Jesus wants to baptize us in His fire and transform us. We must cry out to Him to baptize us with holy fire from heaven so we can be cleansed, filled with His glory and accomplish all of His works. Then we shall be empowered to do greater works than He did.

The Latter Rain

And it shall be that if you earnestly obey My commandments which I command you today, to love the LORD your God and serve Him with all your heart and with all your soul, then I will give you the rain for your land in its season, <u>the early rain and the latter rain</u>, that you may gather in your grain, your new wine, and your oil. And I will send grass in your fields for your livestock, that you may eat and be filled. Take heed to yourselves, lest your heart be deceived, and you turn aside and serve other gods and worship them, lest the LORD's anger be aroused against you, and He shut up the heavens so that there be no rain, and the land yield no produce, and you perish quickly from the good land which the LORD is giving you. Deuteronomy 11:13-17

God's Law gave us a principle and a prophetic picture. Rain is a picture of the blessings of God through the outpouring of His Spirit. There is a former natural rain to enable the planted seed to spring forth and a natural latter rain to bring the harvest unto maturity. As the people of God listened to God's voice and obeyed Him, the Lord promised to send the former and latter rains so that they would have His blessing and prosperity.

Under the New Covenant in Christ Jesus, the same principle applies with a spiritual application. The risen Lord Jesus told His disciples to wait in Jerusalem for the outpouring of the Holy Spirit (Acts 1:4-8). They obeyed His voice and tarried with 120 saints. The spiritual "former rain" came at the day of Pentecost where the seed of Christ was planted in the birthing of His Church (Acts 2). The growth was supernatural and the seed quickly sprouted. The former rain brought supernatural growth so that in two days there were 8,000 new believers. Within a few years the whole ancient world was turned upside down. The outpouring of former rain came down as believers earnestly sought the Lord, heard in faith, obeyed His voice and then prayed in the "rain." The rain manifested in the natural realm in many ways including the gifts of the Holy Spirit, salvations, healings, miracles, signs and wonders.

There is a latter day outpouring of unprecedented magnitude that is coming to mature the Church to a place where she can harvest millions of souls to honor and glorify the sacrifice of God's son. That latter day outpouring is at hand. The glory of the latter house will be far greater than the glory of the former house (Haggai 2:9).

The latter day outpouring of God's Spirit will also be a judgment upon those who have contended with God's people in the Promised Land of their inheritance. As Deborah, Barak and the ten thousand rushed down Mount Tabor to engage Sisera's army, the Lord sent a powerful rainstorm. This was a blessing to God's people and a curse on His enemies. So shall it be in the last days.

God has promised to send His latter day rain. We must seek Him with all our hearts, battle to know Him through the resistance, hear His voice, obey Him and pray in faith to bring in that latter rain outpouring. This spiritual downpour will give mature women of faith incredible prophetic authority, supernatural spiritual gifts and great power. Great levels of power will only be given to vessels purified by fire who have learned to obey God's voice in everything.

God intends that we experience the showers of His blessings in full anointing and power so that we can go forth, out of our captivities, bind the strong man and plunder his goods in the nations. Billions of souls are in captivity to Satan. Jabin and Sisera have controlled and oppressed the people of God to keep them from the great harvest. We need the outpouring of the Holy Spirit to empower us to overcome the enemy.

As we search for God with all our hearts and deal with the flesh and receive impartation of faith we will hear God's voice as Deborah did and follow the Holy Spirit. The prayer of faith will bring the rain, the blessings of God's inheritance into the natural realm where He will empower us to overthrow our enemies and go forth to conquer the nations with an evangelistic thrust unprecedented in history.

This anointed apostolic move of the Holy Spirit will be led by many women who allow themselves to be consumed by the zeal of Elijah and move in violent action to take possession of what God has promised them. One of the results of this great outpouring will be the release of an army of women apostolic evangelists who will be able to pray in the outpouring of the Holy Spirit wherever they go. This is seen in two important passages in the Old Testament.

Many Women Evangelists Shall Go Forth

The voice of one crying in the wilderness: "Prepare the way of the LORD; make straight in the desert a highway for our God. Every valley shall be exalted and every mountain and hill brought low; the crooked places shall

be made straight and the rough places smooth; the glory of the LORD shall be revealed, and all flesh shall see it together; for the mouth of the LORD has spoken."

The voice said, "Cry out!" And he said, "What shall I cry?" "All flesh is grass, and all its loveliness is like the flower of the field. The grass withers, the flower fades, because the breath of the LORD blows upon it; surely the people are grass. The grass withers, the flower fades, but the word of our God stands forever."

O Zion, you who bring good tidings, get up into the high mountain; O Jerusalem, you who bring good tidings, lift up your voice with strength, lift it up, be not afraid; say to the cities of Judah, "Behold your God!"

Behold, the Lord GOD shall come with a strong hand, and His arm shall rule for Him; behold, His reward is with Him, and His work before Him. He will feed His flock like a shepherd; He will gather the lambs with His arm, and carry them in His bosom, and gently lead those who are with young. Isaiah 40:3-11

We immediately recognize that John the Baptist used this passage to identify His ministry as a **"voice crying in the wilderness."** The spirit and power of Elijah will come so that we will be anointed to zealously seek the Lord as Deborah, Elijah and John did. As we seek the Lord and pray in the latter rain, the glory of the Lord shall be revealed to all mankind in the last days.

In Isaiah 40:9-11 and Psalm 68:11, which we shall examine below, the Hebrew verb form of the verb to "bring good tidings" is "lebasser," which is in the feminine form rather than in the more usual masculine form as it is in Naham 1:15; Isaiah 41:27; 52:7. The context of John the Baptist's preparation ministry includes an exhortation for women to rise up and proclaim good news demonstrated by signs and wonders. Dr. Gary Grieg translated this passage as follows with notes on the Hebrew grammar:

"Go up (imperative feminine singular) **on a high mountain, O woman who brings good tidings** (feminine singular participle) **to Zion. Lift up** (imperative feminine singular) **your** (feminine singular) **voice loudly, O woman who brings good tidings** (feminine singular participle) **to Jerusalem. Lift it up** (imperative feminine singular), **do not be afraid** (imperative feminine singular)**! Say** (imperative feminine singular) **to the towns of Judah, "Here is your God!" See, the Sovereign LORD is coming with power, and his strong-arm rules for Him. See, His reward is with Him, and His recompense goes before Him. He is tending His flocks like a shepherd: He is gathering the lambs in his arms and is carrying them on His chest: He is leading those that have young"** (Isaiah 40:9-11).

This passage consistently identifies the evangelist as a female. This does prophesy to the Church, but it clearly affirms the apostolic and evangelistic authority of women who walk in the extraordinary power of the Lord's anointing. These women will also be pure shepherds nurturing their converts as a tender mother nurses her own children.

The Lord giveth the word: the women that publish the tidings are a great host. Kings of armies flee, they flee; and she that tarrieth at home divideth the spoil. Psalms 68:11-12 ASV

The American Standard Version translated the feminine plural participle "lebassar" correctly. A great host of women will be raised up to preach the gospel with extraordinary power. As in Deborah's warfare, kings of armies will flee from these anointed women as rivers of living water are released from their intercession. Women, like Jael, who stay at home and mind the duties of the tent will be powerful intercessors who will share in the rewards. Their prophetic intercession will empower the Deborahs who are released on the field of battle.

Awake O Deborah and Sing

**Awake, awake, Deborah! Awake, awake, sing a song!
Judges 5:12a**

Deborah's refrain echoes through the ages to the women of the last-day Church. The time has finally come as the third-day Church sun arises for women to receive their commissions from the Lord Jesus Christ. As Jesus told Mary and the other faithful women to go and tell His disciples, the Lord will appear to many women and commission them for great roles in the Church of our day.

It is time for Deborahs to awaken, to rise up and take their place in the government of the house of God. The Lord has taught us that Adam and Eve walked in perfect agreement under the anointing so that "they" could obey God's command to exercise dominion on the earth. They fell from this perfect union, but Christ died to bring us back into that level of harmony and authority.

The Bible consistently teaches us to honor our mothers, learn from their instruction and submit to the anointing God gives them. We recognize that there is no gender bias in the heart of God and that women can become sons of God through faith in Christ Jesus. Jesus honored women and allowed them to minister to Him in ways no man did. Jesus appeared to women first after His resurrection as a prophetic picture of the new form He would come on the "third day."

Paul commended Phoebe and Priscilla as powerful ministers of the Lord. John wrote to a lady elder who had a house church that she led. We examined four controversial passages of Paul and recognized translator bias and understood that specific situations in history do not always apply to all peoples in all cultures at all times. Paul honored women in ministry and received from them even as Jesus did.

We took three full chapters to study the life and

prophetic picture seen in Deborah. What an incredible woman she was! Deborah is a model for women today. Under the anointing of the Holy Spirit, Deborah sang the refrain to women of the 21ˢᵗ century:

**Awake, awake, Deborah! Awake, awake, sing a song!
Judges 5:12a**

In the Hebrew and Greek language to magnify an expression, the word is doubled. Only two words are magnified three times, **"Holy, holy, holy"** (Isaiah 6:3; Revelation 4:8) and **"Woe, woe, woe"** (Revelations 8:13). Under the powerful anointing of a prophet, Deborah exclaimed, "Awake, awake, awake, awake," four times in groups of two. I don't know of another instance in scripture where an exhortation is more imperative.

Deborah looked ahead in the Spirit and saw the day when women would come out of thousands of years of captivity and awaken to take their place of authority, anointing and power in the kingdom of God. These women will shake the heavens and the earth with their prophetic intercession. They will search for God with all their hearts, hear His voice and obey Him. These mighty women will pray the prayers of faith like Elijah and bring in the latter rain of God's glory. They will walk in unprecedented power greater than what Jesus, Peter and Paul walked in so as to proclaim the good news to a lost world (John 14:12-14).

The anointing, once on Deborah, is like a dry bone waiting for God's breath to resurrect it to create a mighty army for the Lord (see Ezekiel 37). All the Old Testament anointings and many new ones are available from God to those who will separate themselves and earnestly seek the Lord as Deborah, Elijah and John did. Will you be a Deborah? Will you hear the voice of the Spirit calling the Deborah Church to awaken? Will you come out of complacency and let the glory of God come upon you? Will you pay whatever price is required to take hold of your birthright and destiny in God? By God's grace I pray you will!

I hear the heart cry of Deborah's prophetic word to the women of today and paraphrase her trumpet blast as follows:

"Awake, awake O women. As an ancient mother in Israel, I prayed through and delivered my nation from idolatry and overwhelming oppression. Wake up ladies! Your challenges are great but so were mine. If I could overcome and govern in the house of God as a woman in an ancient Hebrew culture dominated by men, you can do it in your day. You can overcome! Wake up and start singing the song of ministry that the Lord has given you. Take hold of your God and pray, pray, pray in the latter rain."

We are seeing Deborahs arise in our own home. The Lord gave my wife Glenda and me one beautiful son and five extraordinary daughters. All six of our children are walking in the Spirit and running after God with all their hearts. It is our prayer that our daughters will be a first wave of Deborahs who go out in the power of the Lord to publish the good news to the nations.

When I preached a message recently about John the Baptist and the power of His life, one of my daughters was listening intently. As I gave an altar call, our eyes met and a literal flash of light bolted out of her eyes into the natural realm that startled me. It was like a flash bulb or a sharp laser beam explosion from her eyes to mine. She caught the message by the Spirit and was saying yes and amen. When I talked to her about it later, she said, "I've been asking the Lord to give me the eyes of fire."

The prophecies over this daughter are astounding and she has a passion to win souls in the nations. I believe God will anoint her, as well as our other children, in extraordinary ways as we prepare the way through our fastings, prayers and intensity to violently take hold of what Christ accomplished for us. Deborah was married to Lapidoth, the one with eyes of fire. Our daughter is already becoming so one with the Lord that her eyes are a flame of fire. Our youngest daughter, at nine years old, flowed in such a powerful anointing one Sunday that when she blew on people in the prayer lines they fell under God's power.

Just last night, another teenage daughter was asked to pray at our prayer meeting and went into weeping, travailing intercession that brought every intercessor present to the floor in deep humility. As this young Deborah wept into the carpet, Heaven and Earth was moved by her passion and humility. I could tell many stories of the incredible anointings our children are already walking in, and the oldest is only 23. There is nothing greater for a parent than to watch his children passionately run after God. Our children will out run us by far, but we will do everything we can to pull back the bow of Judah, set the arrows of Ephraim with prophetic blessings on their life and loose them to win nations to Jesus. I exhort you women and men to gird up your loins in the Lord and run the race like Deborah did!

Awake, awake, O mighty Deborahs! Awake, awake, and sing your song!

SELECTED BIBLIOGRAPHY

Cornwall, Judson. **The Exhaustive Dictionary of Bible Names**. North Brunswick: Bridge-Logos, 1998

Douglas, J.D. **The New Bible Dictionary**. Grand Rapids: Eerdmans, 1977

Grieg, Gary S. **The Biblical Foundations of Women Alongside Men in Ministry Advancing God's Kingdom.** Wagner Leadership Institute Paper, 1999

Jacobs, Cindy. **Women of Destiny.** Ventura: Regal, 1998

Jones, Alfred. **Jones' Dictionary of Old Testament Proper Names.** Grand Rapids: Kregel, 1997

Smith, William. **Smith's Bible Dictionary**. Peabody: Hendrickson, 1999

Strong, James. **Strong's Exhaustive Concordance of the Bible**. Nashville: Abingdon Press, 1994

Tenny, Merrill C. **The Zondervan Pictoral Encyclopedia of the Bible**. Grand Rapids: Zondervan, 1975, 1976 – Volumes 1-5

Computer Resources:

Gilbertson, Jim. **PC Study Bible for Windows V3.0**. Seattle: Biblesoft, 1997

Includes: Fausset's Bible Dictionary, Nelson's Bible Dictionary, Englishman's Concordance, Vines Expository Dictionary of Words (Old and New Testament), Thayer's Greek Lexicon, Brown-Driver-Briggs Hebrew Lexicon, Strongs Greek/Hebrew Definitions, Treasury of Scripture Knowledge and Nave's Topical Bible

Printed in the United States
28167LVS00001B/190-441

9 781597 810586